POETICS OF MUSIC

Drawing of Stravinsky by Picasso, 1920.

by

IGOR STRAVINSKY

Poetics of Music

IN THE FORM OF SIX LESSONS

PREFACE BY GEORGE SEFERIS

TRANSLATED BY ARTHUR KNODEL AND INGOLF DAHL

Harvard University Press
Cambridge, Massachusetts and London, England

CONTENTS

Preface by George Seferis

EPILOGUE

PREFACE

GEORGE SEFERIS

If I could freely choose where I should like to have been in the academic year 1939–40, my choice would be a place in the youthful audience of Igor Stravinsky at Harvard College. Perhaps I have inherited something from the tradition of the old medieval guilds. It is in that spirit — of an artisan of a bygone age — that I understand Stravinsky when, praising "Bach's incomparable instrumental writing," he notes that one can smell the resin of his violins and taste the reeds of his oboes.[1] And in this same spirit I venture to say that the precepts of renowned masters may carry as much weight as their creations.

Since his time at Harvard important pages have been added to the corpus of texts dealing with the life and works of the great composer. I have in mind his "Conversations" with Robert Craft, who is performing for Stravinsky the service that the young Eckermann did for Goethe. Even so, I must at once insist that just as the Harvard *Lessons* did

[1] Igor Stravinsky and Robert Craft, *Conversations with Igor Stravinsky* (Doubleday: New York, 1959), p. 31.

not supersede such books as the *Chroniques de ma vie* (Paris 1935), so the *Lessons* are complemented, not outmoded, by the thoughts on music and the recollections that have since been given to us.

These six lectures were delivered in French under the title *Poétique musicale sous forme de six leçons* and belong to the distinguished series of Charles Eliot Norton Lectures on Poetry at Harvard University. The original text was long out of print and unobtainable.

Stravinsky tells us how grateful he was, French not being his native language,[2] that he could check the draft of his text with his friend Paul Valéry. It is a charming picture, this collaboration of two devotees of precision. Equally charming, and instructive, is this other detail that the musician gives us: "Even now, a half-century since I left the Russian-speaking world, I still think in Russian, and speak other languages in translation."[3] It is difficult, I think, for Babel to fit into a soul that is striving for unity.[4]

Stravinsky at Harvard makes me think of Paul Valéry. When I was a student in Paris, around 1922, Valéry meant a great deal to me. And later

[2] Igor Stravinsky and Robert Craft, *Memoirs and Commentaries* (Faber and Faber: London, 1960), p. 74.

[3] Igor Stravinsky and Robert Craft, *Expositions and Development* (Faber and Faber: London, 1962), p. 18.

[4] Igor Stravinsky, *Poetics of Music* (Harvard University Press: Cambridge, Mass., 1970), p. 43.

on, when people my seniors who had known him spoke to me about him I was always moved: they all loved him. I shall never forget one autumn evening in the tiny office of T. S. Eliot at Faber and Faber's the voice of the poet of the *Quartets* ending our conversation about Valéry: "He was so intelligent that he had no ambition at all."

And now, as I pen this simple tribute to a musician of our time whom all my life I have regarded with devotion. I recall the phrase in one of Valéry's letters: " . . . en matière musicale les mots du métier ne me disent rien que de vague ou d'intimidant." I share this feeling and I was very hesitant to agree to write even these few words. And my hesitation was reinforced by Stravinsky's own observation: "How misleading are all literary descriptions of musical form." [5] Indeed yes, and it is not a question simply of music. Generally, I think, it is misleading to transfer a given artistic expression from the medium which gave birth to it to some other which will, inevitably, be alien. I give an example.

We are all familiar with the episode related in Book II of the *Aeneid*, the episode in which the serpents strangle Laocoön and his sons. It would, I fear, be difficult to maintain that either El Greco's painting of the scene (which we admire in the

[5] *Conversations with Igor Stravinsky*, p. 17.

National Gallery in Washington) or the famous Rhodian statue conveys exactly, without misleading, the expression of Virgil's verses. And one could say the same of Stéphane Mallarmé's *Après-midi d'un faune* and Debussy's superb musical setting of the poem. Each art has its own medium, that material which the artist's creative manipulation suddenly and unexpectedly makes more sensitive — molds it into a form different from the way we see it in everyday life. This is a clarification that I feel obliged to make and at the same time it implies a distinction between the use of words as the medium of poetry and the use of words for didactic or explanatory purposes. It is this latter use that one marvels at in Stravinsky, both in his Harvard lectures and in the choice pages with which from time to time he favors us.

Nevertheless, for Stravinsky's most profound expression (and I use the word in an absolute sense) it is not in the realm of words that we must search but in the realm of sound. There he has transfused his whole self, there he has made his mark as a great master of music, a figure comparable in stature to that other pillar of our age, Pablo Picasso. Their works, the expression of these two men, have set their seal on our time, but if one is to find the catharsis, the deliverance, that they offer us it is to the works themselves that we must go, not to intermediary words, the countless words that have been written about them.

I once observed, perhaps in a carefree moment of exaggeration, that even if the language we speak were reduced to a single word the good poet would still be readily distinguished from the poet of lesser talent. Thus I found food for thought in the passage that Stravinsky at the end of the *Lessons* ascribes to the Areopagite: "The greater the dignity of the angels in the celestial hierarchy," says the Saint, "the fewer words they use; so that the most elevated of all pronounces only a single syllable." [6]

A word, a syllable, a single sound. The goal that one strives for but never attains. Yet the road traveled, the long blind way that we easily lose and only with great toil find again, this is what touches us to the quick in the life of the creative artist.

I am grateful to these few lines because they have given me the occasion this past month to hear again — in recordings — a large part of Stravinsky's work and to read his Conversations. In one of these, an interview that reached me just at the right time, [7] he speaks of the last quartets of Beethoven and says: "The quartets are a charter of human rights," and, again, "A high concept of freedom is embodied in the quartets." This view, I must confess, caused

[6] *Poetics of Music*, p. 185.

[7] Igor Stravinsky, "Where is thy sting?", *The New York Review of Books*, 12:4 (April 24, 1969); reprinted in Igor Stravinsky and Robert Craft, *Retrospectives and Conclusions* (Knopf: New York, 1969).

me some malaise. And then, suddenly, I thought of the basic significance that time has for music and for Stravinsky himself: witness the phrase where he speaks of the "natural respiration" of music, his affirmation that "pulsation is the reality of music." [8] At the same moment there flashed into my mind a quartet that has become part of my life and that I have listened to countless times, Opus 132, especially the third movement ("molto adagio") his "Hymn of Thanksgiving in the Lydian mode." Then at last I felt that I saw clearly what Stravinsky meant: music (as he taught us in the second *Lesson*) is the art of time; and also, I reflected, our human bodies are subject to time, this tortured humanity that continually yearns to breathe freely in the radiance of health. Here Mallarmé's "l'ennui de fournir du bavardage" made me halt.

One note more. Out of the rich harvest of facts and gestures of Igor Stravinsky that Robert Craft offers us, one in particular sticks in my mind. Craft remarks: "I have noticed that you always sleep with a light on; do you remember the origin of this need?" Stravinsky replies: "I am able to sleep at night only when a ray of light enters my room from a closet or adjoining chamber . . . The light I still seek to be reminded of must have come . . . from the street lamp outside my window on the Krukov Canal . . . Whatever it was, however . . . this umbilical cord of illumination still enables me at

[8] *Memoirs and Commentaries*, p. 113.

seventy-eight, to re-enter the world of safety and enclosure I knew at seven or eight." [9]

I marvel to hear this from a man who declares bluntly: "I do not like to remember my childhood." [10]

Just the same, that dim but persistent light which first shone from a street lamp of old St. Petersburg and decade after decade, long after its original source must have been extinguished, continued — like the light of a burnt-out star — to illumine his sleep and to provide him the security of childhood.

Last year Stravinsky said: "But I know I have more music in me, nevertheless. And I must give; I cannot live a purely receiving life." [11] God grant him many years to come! And may that gleam from the nocturnal Krukov Canal still attend his fruitful dreams!

Athens, May 1969

[9] *Expositions and Development*, p. 13.
[10] *Memoirs and Conversations*, p. 24.
[11] Igor Stravinsky, "Side Effects: An Interview," *The New York Review of Books*, 10:8 (March 14, 1968); reprinted in Igor Stravinsky and Robert Craft, *Retrospectives and Conclusions* (Knopf: New York, 1969).

1. GETTING ACQUAINTED

CONSIDER IT A GREAT HONOR TO occupy the Charles Eliot Norton chair of poetics today, and I take particular pleasure in thanking the Committee that has so kindly invited me to address the students of Harvard University.

I cannot conceal from you how happy I am to be speaking for the first time to an audience that is willing to take the trouble of listening and learning before judging.

Up to the present I have appeared on the concert platform and in theater-halls before those agglomerations of people that make up what we call the public. But never until today have I addressed an audience of students. As students, undoubtedly eager to acquire solid information about matters that are presented to you, you will not be surprised if I warn you that the particular matter I am going to discuss with you is serious — more serious than is generally thought. I hope you will not be frightened by its density, by its specific gravity. I have no intention of overwhelming you . . . but it is difficult to talk about music if one considers only its material realities; and I should feel I were betraying music if I made it the subject of a dissertation hastily thrown together, sprinkled with anecdotes and amusing digressions.

I shall not forget that I occupy a chair of *poetics*. And it is no secret to any of you that the exact meaning of poetics is the study of work to be done. The verb *poiein* from which the word is derived means nothing else but *to do* or *make*. The poetics of the classical philosophers did not consist of lyrical dissertations about natural talent and about the essence of beauty. For them the single word *techné* embraced both the fine arts and the useful arts and was applied to the knowledge and study of the certain and inevitable rules of the craft. That is why Aristotle's *Poetics* constantly suggest ideas regarding personal work, arrangement of materials, and structure. The poetics of music is exactly what I am going to talk to you about; that is to say, I shall talk about *making* in the field of music. Suffice it to say that we shall not use music as a pretext for pleasant fancies. For myself, I am too much aware of the responsibility incumbent upon me not to take my task seriously.

So if I greatly prize the advantage I have in speaking before you who are here to study and to get from me whatever I may be capable of giving, you, in return, will, I hope, enjoy the advantage of actually being witnesses of a series of musical confessions.

Do not be alarmed. They will not be confessions of the Jean Jacques Rousseau sort, and even less of the psychoanalytic sort which, under a pseudo-scientific

4

guise, merely effect a sad profanation of man's real values and of his psychological and creative faculties.

I should like to place my plan of confessions midway between an *academic* course (and may I call your attention to this term, because I shall refer to it again in the course of my lessons) and what one might call an *apology* for my own general ideas. I use the word apology not in its current French sense, where it means eulogy, but in the sense of a justification and defense of my ideas and personal views. In fine, all this means that I shall be giving you dogmatic confidences.

I am fully aware that the words *dogma* and *dogmatic*, however sparingly one may apply them to aesthetic matters or even to spiritual matters, never fail to offend — even to shock — certain mentalities richer in sincerity than they are strong in certitudes. For that very reason I insist all the more that you accept these terms to the full extent of their legitimate meaning, and I would advise you to recognize their validity, to become familiar with them; and hope that you will come to develop a taste for them. If I speak of the legitimate meaning of these terms, it is to emphasize the normal and natural use of the dogmatic element in any field of activity in which it becomes categorical and truly essential.

In fact, we cannot observe the creative phenomenon independently of the form in which it is made manifest. Every formal process proceeds from a principle, and the study of this principle requires precisely what we call dogma. In other words, the need that we feel

5

to bring order out of chaos, to extricate the straight line of our operation from the tangle of possibilities and from the indecision of vague thoughts, presupposes the necessity of some sort of dogmatism. I use the words *dogma* and *dogmatic*, then, only insofar as they designate an element essential to safeguarding the integrity of art and mind, and I maintain that in this context they do not usurp their function.

The very fact that we have recourse to what we call *order* — that order which permits us to dogmatize in the field we are considering — not only develops our taste for dogmatism: it incites us to place our own creative activity under the aegis of dogmatism. That is why I should like to see you accept the term.

Throughout my course and on every hand I shall call upon your feeling and your taste for order and discipline. For they — fed, informed, and sustained by positive concepts — form the basis of what is called dogma.

For the moment, to guide you in the organization of your future studies, I must advise you that my course is to be limited to the development of theses that will constitute an explanation of music in lesson form. Why do I use the word *explanation*? And just why do I speak of *an* explanation? Because what I intend to say to you will not constitute an impersonal exposition of general data, but will be an explanation of music as I conceive it. Nor will this explanation be any the less objective for being the fruit of my own experience and my personal observations.

6

The fact that the value and efficacy of such an explanation have been tested in my own experience convinces me — and guarantees you — that I am not offering you a mass of mere opinions, but rather that I am submitting to you a body of findings which, though made by me, are none the less just as valid for others as for myself.

Thus, it is not a question of my private feelings and tastes; nor is it a question of a theory of music projected through a subjective prism. My experiences and investigations are entirely objective, and my introspections have led me to question myself only that I might derive something concrete from them.

These ideas that I am developing, these causes that I am defending and that I have been brought before you to defend in a systematic fashion, have served and will continue to serve as the basis for musical creation precisely because they have been developed in actual practice. And if you attribute any importance, however slight, to my creative work — which is the fruit of my conscience and my faith — then please give credit to the speculative concepts that have engendered my work and that have developed along with it.

To explain — or, in French, to explicate, from the Latin *explicare*, to unfold, to develop — is to describe something, to discover its genesis, to note the relationship of things to each other, to seek to throw light upon them. To explain myself to you is also to explain myself to myself and to be obliged to clear up matters that are distorted or betrayed by the ignorance and malevolence that one always finds united by some mysterious bond in most of the judgments that are passed upon the arts. Ignorance and malevolence are united in a single root; the latter benefits surreptitiously from the advantages it draws from the former. I do not know which is the more hateful. In itself ignorance is, of course, no crime. It begins to be suspect when it pleads sincerity; for sincerity, as Rémy de Gourmont said, is hardly an explanation and is never an excuse. And malevolence never fails to plead ignorance as an attenuating circumstance.

It will be readily granted that this shady collusion of "ignorance, infirmity, and malice" — to use the language of theology — justifies a rebuttal, a loyal and vigorous defense. That is how I understand the term "polemic."

So I am obliged to be polemical. First, in view of the subversion of musical values that I have just referred to and, secondly, in defense of a cause that may appear to be a personal one at first glance, but which in reality is not. Let me explain this second point: by some chance, which it pleases me to regard as a happy one, my person and my work have in spite of myself been stamped with a distinctive mark from the outset of my career and have played the part of a "reagent." The contact of this reagent with the musical reality around me, with human environments and the world of ideas, has provoked various reactions whose violence has been equalled only by arbitrariness. It seems that everyone had the wrong address. But above and beyond my own work, these unthinking reactions have affected music as a whole and revealed the seriousness of a flaw in judgment that vitiated the musical consciousness of a whole epoch and invalidated all ideas, theses, and opinions that were put forth concerning one of the highest faculties of the spirit — music as an art. Let us not forget that *Petrouchka*, the *Rite of Spring*, and the *Nightingale* appeared at a time characterized by profound changes that dislocated many things and troubled many minds. Not that these changes took place in the domain of aesthetics or on the level of modes of expression (that sort of upheaval had taken place at an earlier time, at the outset of my activities). The changes of which I speak effected a general revision of both the basic values and the primordial elements of the art of music.

This revision, first apparent at the time I just spoke of, has continued unabated ever since. What I am here stating is self-evident and is clearly to be read from the unfolding of concrete facts and daily events we are now witnessing.

I am well aware that there is a point of view that regards the period in which the *Rite of Spring* appeared as one that witnessed a revolution. A revolution whose conquests are said to be in the process of assimilation today. I deny the validity of that opinion. I hold that it was wrong to have considered me a revolutionary. When the *Rite* appeared, many opinions were advanced concerning it. In the tumult of contradictory opinions my friend Maurice Ravel intervened practically alone to set matters right. He was able to see, and he said, that the novelty of the *Rite* consisted, not in the "writing," not in the orchestration, not in the technical apparatus of the work, but in the musical entity.

I was made a revolutionary in spite of myself. Now, revolutionary outbreaks are never completely spontaneous. There are clever people who bring about revolutions with malice aforethought . . . It is always necessary to guard against being misrepresented by those who impute to you an intention that is not your own. For myself, I never hear anyone talk about revolution without thinking of the conversation that G. K. Chesterton tells us he had, on landing in France, with a Calais innkeeper. The innkeeper complained bitterly of the harshness of life and the increasing lack of freedom: " 'It's hardly worth while,' concluded the innkeeper, 'to have had three revolutions only to end up every time just where you started.' " Whereupon Chesterton pointed out to him that a revolution, in the true sense of the word, was the movement of an object in motion that described a closed curve, and thus always returned to the point from where it had started . . .

The tone of a work like the *Rite* may have appeared arrogant, the language that it spoke may have seemed harsh in its newness, but that in no way implies that it is revolutionary in the most subversive sense of the word.

If one only need break a habit to merit being

labeled revolutionary, then every musician who has something to say and who in order to say it goes beyond the bounds of established convention would be known as revolutionary. Why burden the dictionary of the fine arts with this stertorous term, which designates in its most usual acceptation a state of turmoil and violence, when there are so many other words better adapted to designate originality?

In truth, I should be hard pressed to cite for you a single fact in the history of art that might be qualified as revolutionary. Art is by essence constructive. Revolution implies a disruption of equilibrium. To speak of revolution is to speak of a temporary chaos. Now art is the contrary of chaos. It never gives itself up to chaos without immediately finding its living works, its very existence, threatened.

The quality of being revolutionary is generally attributed to artists in our day with a laudatory intent, undoubtedly because we are living in a period when revolution enjoys a kind of prestige among yesterday's elite. Let us understand each other: I am the first to recognize that daring is the motive force of the finest and greatest acts; which is all the more reason for not putting it unthinkingly at the service of disorder and base cravings in a desire to cause sensation at any price. I approve of daring; I set no limits to it. But likewise there are no limits to the mischief wrought by arbitrary acts.

To enjoy to the full the conquests of daring, we must demand that it operate in a pitiless light. We are work-

11

ing in its favor when we denounce the false wares that would usurp its place. Gratuitous excess spoils every substance, every form that it touches. In its blundering it impairs the effectiveness of the most valuable discoveries and at the same time corrupts the taste of its devotees — which explains why their taste often plunges without transition from the wildest complications to the flattest banalities.

A musical complex, however harsh it may be, is legitimate to the extent to which it is genuine. But to recognize genuine values in the midst of the excesses of sham one must be gifted with a sure instinct that our snobs hate all the more intensely for being themselves completely deprived thereof.

Our vanguard elite, sworn perpetually to outdo itself, expects and requires that music should satisfy the taste for absurd cacophony.

I say *cacophony* without fear of being classed with the ranks of conventional *pompiers*, the *laudatores temporis acti*. And in using the word I am certain I am not in the least reversing myself. My position in this regard is exactly the same as it was at the time when I composed the *Rite* and when people saw fit to call me a revolutionary. Today, just as in the past, I am on my guard against counterfeit money and take care not to accept it for the true coin of the realm. Cacophony means bad sound, contraband merchandise, uncoördinated music that will not stand up under serious criticism. Whatever opinion one may hold about the music of Arnold Schoenberg (to take as an example a composer evolving along lines essentially different from mine, both aesthetically and technically), whose works have frequently given rise to violent reactions or ironic smiles — it is impossible for a self-respecting mind equipped with genuine musical culture not to feel that the composer of *Pierrot Lunaire* is fully aware of what he is doing and that he is not trying to deceive anyone. He adopted the musical system that suited his needs and, within this system, he is perfectly consistent with himself, perfectly coherent. One cannot dismiss music that he dislikes by labeling it cacophony.

Equally degrading is the vanity of snobs who boast of an embarrassing familiarity with the world of the incomprehensible and who delightedly confess that they find themselves in good company. It is not music they seek, but rather the effect of shock, the sensation that befuddles understanding.

So I confess that I am completely insensitive to the prestige of revolution. All the noise it may make will not call forth the slightest echo in me. For revolution is one thing, innovation another. And even innovation, when not presented in an excessive form, is not always recognized by its contemporaries. Let me take as an example the work of a composer whom I choose purposely because his music, the qualities of which have long been clearly recognized, has become so universally popular that barrel-organs everywhere have made it their own.

I am speaking of Charles Gounod. Don't be surprised at my lingering over Gounod for a moment. It is not so much the composer of *Faust* who holds my attention as it is the example that Gounod offers us of a work whose most obvious merits were misunderstood when they were still new by the very people whose mission it is to be exactly informed about the realities they have to judge.

Take *Faust*. The first critics of this famous opera refused to acknowledge in Gounod the melodic inventiveness that today seems to us the dominant trait of his talent. They even went so far as to question whether he had any melodic gift at all. They saw in Gounod "a symphonist astray in the theater," a "severe musician," to use their own terms, and, of course, more "learned" than "inspired." Naturally, they reproached him with having "achieved his effects not through the voices, but through the orchestra."

In 1862, three years after the first performances of *Faust*, the *Gazette musicale* of Paris declared quite flatly that *Faust*, as a whole, "was not the work of a melodist." As for the famous Scudo whose word was law for the *Revue des Deux Mondes*, this Scudo in the same year turned out the following historical masterpiece, which I should never forgive myself for not quoting to you in full:

Monsieur Gounod, to his misfortune, admires certain outmoded portions of Beethoven's last quartets. They constitute the muddied wellspring from which issue the bad musicians of modern Germany: the Liszts, the Wagners, the Schumanns, and even Mendelssohn in certain questionable aspects of his style. If Monsieur Gounod has really made his own the doctrine of continuous melody, of the melody of the virgin forest and of the setting sun, that constitutes the charm of *Tannhäuser* and of *Lohengrin*, a melody that may be compared to Harlequin's letter: "as for periods and commas, I don't give them a thought, I leave it to you to put them wherever you wish" — Monsieur Gounod in that case, which I should like to believe impossible, will be irrevocably lost.

But even the Germans corroborated the good Scudo after their fashion. As a matter of fact, one could read in the *Münchener Neueste Nachrichten* that Gounod wasn't French, but Belgian, and that his compositions did not bear the stamp of the contemporary French and Italian schools but precisely that of the German school in which he had been educated and formed.

Since the literature that springs up on every side of music has not changed in the last seventy years and since, while music is constantly changing, the commentators who refuse to take note of these transformations do not themselves change — we must naturally take up cudgels.

Therefore, I am going to be polemical. I am not afraid to admit this. I shall be polemical not in my own defense, but in order to defend in words all music and its principles, just as I defend them in a different way with my compositions.

And now let me explain to you how my course is organized. It will be divided into six lessons, each of which shall have a separate title.

The lesson that I have just presented to you, as you can readily see, is only a means of our *getting acquainted* with one another. In this first lesson I have tried to summarize the guiding principles of my course. You know now that you are going to hear musical confessions, and you know what meaning I attach to that expression and how the apparently subjective character of the word is counteracted by my desire to give a clearly dogmatic character to these confidences.

Our introduction to each other under the stern auspices of order and discipline should not frighten you, since my course will not be limited to an arid and impersonal exposition of general ideas but will comprise as vital as possible an explanation of music as I understand it; an explanation of my personal experience, faithfully related to concrete values.

My second lesson will take up the phenomenon of music. I shall leave aside the insoluble problem of the origins of music in order to dwell upon the musical phenomenon in itself, insofar as it emanates from a complete and well-balanced human being endowed with the resources of his senses and armed with his intellect. We shall study the phenomenon of music as a form of speculation in terms of sound and time. We shall derive from this study the dialectics of the creative process. In this connection I shall speak to you of the principle of contrast and similarity. The second part of that lesson will be devoted to the elements and the morphology of music.

The composing of music will be the subject matter

of my third lesson. In it we shall consider the following questions: What is composition, and what is the composer? Just how and to what degree is the composer a creator? These considerations will lead us to study one by one the formal elements of the craft of music. In this connection we shall have to make very explicit the concepts of invention, imagination, inspiration; of culture and taste; of order as rule and as law opposed to disorder; and finally the opposition of the realm of necessity to the realm of freedom.

The fourth lesson will take up musical typology studied through an inspection of its historical origins and development. Typology presupposes an act of selection which presumes a certain method of discrimination. The analyses which this method prompts us to make will bring us to the problem of style and beyond that to the play of formal elements, whose unfolding constitutes what might be called the biography of music. During the course of this lesson I shall examine a number of questions that vitally concern us today: those that involve the public, snobbery, patronage, and philistinism. Likewise modernism and academicism and the eternal question of classicism and romanticism.

The fifth lesson will be entirely devoted to Russian music. In connection with it I shall take up folklore and Russian musical culture; plain song and music both sacred and profane. I shall also speak about the Italianism, Germanism, and orientalism of nineteenth century Russian music. I shall call to mind the two disorders of the two Russias — the conservative and

17

the revolutionary disorders. Finally, I shall speak to you about the neo-folklorism of the Soviets and of the degrading of musical values.

The sixth and last lesson, which will take up actual performance, will lead me to a description of the physical phenomenon of music. I shall establish the elements that distinguish interpretation from execution properly speaking, and in this regard I shall also speak of performers and their listeners, of the activity and passivity of the audience as well as of the all-important problem of judgment or criticism. My epilogue will seek to determine the profound meaning of music and its essential aim, which is to promote a communion, a union of man with his fellow-man and with the Supreme Being.

As you see, this *explanation* of music that I am going to undertake for you and, I hope, with you, will assume the form of a synthesis, of a system that will begin with an analysis of the phenomenon of music and terminate with the problem of the performing of music. You will note that I have not chosen the method most frequently applied in syntheses of this sort: the method which develops a thesis by proceeding from the general to the particular. I shall go about it differently. I shall adopt a sort of parallelism, a method of *synchronization*; that is, I shall link up general principles with particular facts, constantly supporting the one with the other.

For it should be recognized that it is only by reason of a practical necessity that we are obliged to differentiate things by arranging them in purely conventional categories such as "primary and secondary," "principal and subordinate." Besides, my aim is not to separate the elements that concern us, but to single them out without disuniting them.

The true hierarchy of phenomena, as well as the true hierarchy of relationships, takes on substance and form on a plane entirely apart from that of conventional classifications.

Let me entertain the hope that the clarification of this thesis will be one of the results of my course, a result I greatly desire.

2. THE PHENOMENON OF MUSIC

I SHALL TAKE THE MOST BANAL example: that of the pleasure we experience on hearing the murmur of the breeze in the trees, the rippling of a brook, the song of a bird. All this pleases us, diverts us, delights us. We may even say: "What lovely music!" Naturally, we are speaking only in terms of comparison. But then, *comparison* is not *reason*. These natural sounds suggest music to us, but are not yet themselves music. If we take pleasure in these sounds by imagining that on being exposed to them we become musicians and even, momentarily, creative musicians, we must admit that we are fooling ourselves. They are promises of music; it takes a human being to keep them: a human being who is sensitive to nature's many voices, of course, but who in addition feels the need of putting them in order and who is gifted for that task with a very special aptitude. In his hands all that I have considered as not being music will become music. From this I conclude that tonal elements become music only by virtue of their being organized, and that such organization presupposes a conscious human act.

23

Thus I take cognizance of the existence of elemental natural sounds, the raw materials of music, which, pleasing in themselves, may caress the ear and give us a pleasure that may be quite complete. But, over and beyond this passive enjoyment we shall discover music, music that will make us participate actively in the working of a mind that orders, gives life, and creates. For at the root of all creation one discovers an appetite that is not an appetite for the fruits of the earth. So that to the gifts of nature are added the benefits of artifice — such is the general significance of art.

For it is not art that rains down upon us in the song of a bird; but the simplest modulation correctly executed is already art, without any possible doubt.

Art in the true sense is a way of fashioning works according to certain methods acquired either by apprenticeship or by inventiveness. And methods are the straight and predetermined channels that insure the rightness of our operation.

There is a historical perspective that, like every view of things which is subordinated to the laws of optical perspective, only renders distinct those objects on the nearest planes. As the planes recede from us, they elude our grasp and only let us catch glimpses of objects devoid of life and useful meaning. A thousand obstacles separate us from the ancestral riches which yield to us only aspects of their dead reality. And even then we grasp them by intuition rather than by conscious knowing.

Hence, in order to lay hold of the phenomenon of

music at its origins, there is no need to study primitive rituals, modes of incantation, or to penetrate the secrets of ancient magic. To have recourse to history in this case — even to prehistory — is that not to overshoot our mark by seeking to grasp what cannot be grasped? How shall we reasonably explain what no one has ever witnessed? If we take reason alone as a guide in this field, it will lead us straight to falsehoods, since it will no longer be enlightened by instinct. Instinct is infallible. If it leads us astray, it is no longer instinct. At all events, a living illusion is more valuable in such matters than a dead reality.

One day the *Comédie française* was rehearsing a medieval play in which the celebrated actor Mounet-Sully, according to the author's directions, had to swear an oath on an old Bible. For rehearsals the old Bible had been replaced by a telephone directory. "The script calls for an old Bible," roared Mounet-Sully. "Get me an old Bible!" Jules Claretie, the director of the *Comédie*, promptly rushed into his library to find a copy of the two testaments in a magnificent old edition and brought it triumphantly to the actor. "Here you are, *mon cher Doyen*," said Claretie, "a fifteenth century edition . . ." "Fifteenth century!" said Mounet-Sully. "But then at that time it was brand new . . ."

Mounet-Sully was right, if you insist. But he attributed too much importance to archaeology.

The past slips from our grasp. It leaves us only scattered things. The bond that united them eludes us.

Our imagination usually fills in the void by making use of preconceived theories. In this way, for example, a materialist appeals to Darwin's theories in placing the monkey before man in the evolution of animal species.

Archaeology, then, does not supply us with certitudes, but rather with vague hypotheses. And in the shade of these hypotheses some artists are content to dream, considering them less as scientific facts than as sources of inspiration. This is just as true of music as of the plastic arts. Painters of every period, including our own, let their fancies roam through time and space and offer sacrifices successively or even simultaneously on the altars of archaism and exoticism.

Such a tendency in itself calls neither for praise nor censure. Let us merely note that these imaginary voyages supply us with nothing that is exact and do not make us better acquainted with music.

In our first lesson we were astonished to find that, in the case of Gounod, sixty-nine years ago even *Faust* at first encountered listeners who rebelled against the charm of its melody and were insensitive and deaf to its originality.

What then shall we say about ancient music, and how could we judge it with the instrument of our reasoning mind alone? For here instinct fails us. We lack an indispensable element of investigation: namely, the sensation of the music itself.

My own experience has long convinced me that any historical fact, recent or distant, may well be utilized as a stimulus to set the creative faculty in motion, but never as an aid for clearing up difficulties.

One builds solidly only on the bedrock of the immediate, because what is no longer in use can no longer serve us directly. So it is futile to go back beyond a certain point to data that no longer permit us to contemplate the music itself.

In fact, we must not forget that music of the kind that has meaning for us today is the youngest of all the arts, although its origins may be as old as man's. When we go back beyond the fourteenth century material difficulties stop us short and pile up to such an extent that we are reduced to making conjectures when we come to decipher it.

For myself, I cannot begin to take an interest in the phenomenon of music except insofar as it emanates from the integral man. I mean from a man armed with the resources of his senses, his psychological faculties, and his intellectual equipment.

Only the integral man is capable of the effort of higher speculation that must now occupy our attention.

For the phenomenon of music is nothing other than a phenomenon of speculation. There is nothing in this expression that should frighten you. It simply presupposes that the basis of musical creation is a preliminary feeling out, a will moving first in an abstract realm with the object of giving shape to something concrete. The elements at which this speculation necessarily aims are those of *sound* and *time*. Music is inconceivable apart from those two elements.

27

To facilitate our exposition, we shall first speak about time.

The plastic arts are presented to us in space: we receive an over-all impression before we'discover details little by little and at our leisure. But music is based on temporal succession and requires alertness of memory. Consequently music is a *chronologic* art, as painting is a *spatial* art. Music presupposes before all else a certain organization in time, a chrononomy — if you will permit me to use a neologism.

The laws that regulate the movement of sounds require the presence of a measurable and constant value: *meter*, a purely material element, through which rhythm, a purely formal element, is realized. In other words, meter answers the question of how many equal parts the musical unit which we call a measure is to be divided into, and rhythm answers the question of how these equal parts will be grouped within a given measure. A measure in four beats, for example, may be composed of two groups of two beats, or in three groups: one beat, two beats, and one beat, and so on . . .

Thus we see that meter, since it offers in itself only elements of symmetry and is inevitably made up of even quantities, is necessarily utilized by rhythm, whose function it is to establish order in the movement by dividing up the quantities furnished in the measure.

Who of us, on hearing jazz music, has not felt an amusing sensation approaching giddiness when a dancer or a solo musician, trying persistently to stress irregular accents, cannot succeed in turning our ear away from the regular pulsation of the meter drummed out by the percussion?

How do we react to an impression of this sort? What strikes us most in this conflict of rhythm and meter? It is the obsession with regularity. The isochronous beats are in this case merely a means of throwing the rhythmic invention of the soloist into relief. It is this that brings about surprise and produces the unexpected. On reflection we realize that without the real or implied presence of the beats we could not make out the meaning of this invention. Here we are enjoying a relationship.

This example seems to me to clarify sufficiently the connections between meter and rhythm, in the hierarchical sense as well as in the chrononomic sense.

What are we to say, now that we are fully informed, when someone talks — as is too often the case — about a "fast rhythm"? How can such a blunder be made by a reasonable person? For after all, speeding up only alters movement. If I sing the American national anthem twice as fast as usual, I modify its *tempo*; in no way do I change its rhythm, since the relationship of note values remains intact.

I have made it a point to spend a few minutes on this very elementary question because one sees it strangely distorted by ignorant persons who singularly abuse the vocabulary of music.

More complex and really fundamental is the specific problem of musical time, of the *chronos* of music. This problem has recently been made the object of a particularly interesting study by Mr. Pierre Souvtchinsky, a Russian philosopher-friend of mine. His thinking is so closely akin to mine that I can do no better than to summarize his thesis here.

Musical creation appears to him an innate complex of intuitions and possibilities based primarily upon an exclusively musical experiencing of time — *chronos*, of which the musical work merely gives us the functional realization.

Everyone knows that time passes at a rate which varies according to the inner dispositions of the subject and to the events that come to affect his consciousness. Expectation, boredom, anguish, pleasure and pain, contemplation — all of these thus come to appear as different categories in the midst of which our life unfolds, and each of these determines a special psychological process, a particular tempo. These variations in psychological time are perceptible only as they are related to the primary sensation — whether conscious or unconscious — of real time, ontological time.

What gives the concept of musical time its special stamp is that this concept is born and develops as well outside of the categories of psychological time as it does simultaneously with them. All music, whether it submits to the normal flow of time, or whether it disassociates itself therefrom, establishes a particular relationship, a sort of counterpoint between the passing of time, the music's own duration, and the material and technical means through which the music is made manifest.

Mr. Souvtchinsky thus presents us with two kinds of music: one which evolves parallel to the process of ontological time, embracing and penetrating it, inducing in the mind of the listener a feeling of euphoria and, so to speak, of "dynamic calm." The other kind runs ahead of, or counter to, this process. It is not self-contained in each momentary tonal unit. It dislocates the centers of attraction and gravity and sets itself up in the unstable; and this fact makes it particularly adaptable to the translation of the composer's emotive impulses. All music in which the will to expression is dominant belongs to the second type.

This problem of time in the art of music is of capital importance. I have thought it wise to dwell on the problem because the considerations that it involves may help us to understand the different creative types which will concern us in our fourth lesson.

Music that is based on ontological time is generally dominated by the principle of similarity. The music that adheres to psychological time likes to proceed by contrast. To these two principles which dominate the creative process correspond the fundamental concepts of variety and unity.

All the arts have recourse to this principle. The methods of polychromatics and monochromatics in the plastic arts correspond respectively to variety and unity. For myself, I have always considered that in general it is more satisfactory to proceed by similarity rather than by contrast. Music thus gains strength in the measure that it does not succumb to the seductions of variety. What it loses in questionable riches it gains in true solidity.

Contrast produces an immediate effect. Similarity satisfies us only in the long run. Contrast is an element of variety, but it divides our attention. Similarity is born of a striving for unity. The need to seek variety is perfectly legitimate, but we should not forget that the One precedes the Many. Moreover, the coexistence of both is constantly necessary, and all the problems of art, like all possible problems for that matter, including the problem of knowledge and of Being, revolve ineluctably about this question, with Parmenides on one side denying the possibility of the Many, and Heraclitus on the other denying the existence of the One. Mere common sense, as well as supreme wisdom, invite us to affirm both the one and the other. All the same, the best attitude for a composer in this case will be the attitude of a man who is conscious of the hierarchy of values and who must make a choice. Variety is valid only as a means of attaining similarity. Variety surrounds me on every hand. So I need not fear that I shall be lacking in it, since I am constantly confronted by it. Contrast is everywhere. One has only to take note of it. Similarity is hidden; it must be sought out, and it is found only after the most exhaustive efforts. When variety tempts me, I am uneasy about the facile solutions it offers me. Similarity, on the other hand, poses more difficult problems but also offers results

32

that are more solid and hence more valuable to me.

Needless to say, we have not exhausted this eternal subject here, and we shall want to return to it.

We are not in a conservatory, and I have no intention of bothering you with musical pedagogy. It is not my concern at this point to bring up certain elementary principles which are known to most of you and which, if need be — supposing that you may have forgotten them — you would find clearly set forth in any textbook. I shall not detain you with the concepts of intervals, chords, modes, harmony, modulation, register, and timbre — none of which are at all ambiguous; but I shall dwell for a moment on certain elements of musical terminology that may lead to confusion, and I shall try to clear up certain misunderstandings, as I have just done in regard to the *chronos* by speaking about meter and rhythm.

All of you know that the range of audible sounds constitutes the physical basis of the art of music. You also know that the scale is formed by means of the tones of the harmonic series arranged in diatonic order in a succession different from the one that nature offers us.

You likewise know that the pitch relationship between two tones is called an interval, and that a chord is the sound-complex that results from the simultaneous sounding of at least three tones of a different pitch.

All is well up to this point, and all this is clear to

us. But the concepts of consonance and dissonance have given rise to tendentious interpretations that should definitely be set aright.

Consonance, says the dictionary, is the combination of several tones into an harmonic unit. Dissonance results from the deranging of this harmony by the addition of tones foreign to it. One must admit that all this is not clear. Ever since it appeared in our vocabulary, the word dissonance has carried with it a certain odor of sinfulness.

Let us light our lantern: in textbook language, dissonance is an element of transition, a complex or interval of tones which is not complete in itself and which must be resolved to the ear's satisfaction into a perfect consonance.

But just as the eye completes the lines of a drawing which the painter has knowingly left incomplete, just so the ear may be called upon to complete a chord and coöperate in its resolution, which has not actually been realized in the work. Dissonance, in this instance, plays the part of an allusion.

Either case applies to a style where the use of dissonance demands the necessity of a resolution. But nothing forces us to be looking constantly for satisfaction that resides only in repose. And for over a century music has provided repeated examples of a style in which dissonance has emancipated itself. It is no longer tied down to its former function. Having become an entity in itself, it frequently happens that dissonance neither prepares nor anticipates anything. Dissonance is thus no more an agent of disorder than consonance is a guarantee of security. The music of yesterday and of today unhesitatingly unites parallel dissonant chords that thereby lose their functional value, and our ear quite naturally accepts their juxtaposition.

Of course, the instruction and education of the public have not kept pace with the evolution of technique. The use of dissonance, for ears ill-prepared to accept it, has not failed to confuse their reaction, bringing about a state of debility in which the dissonant is no longer distinguished from the consonant.

We thus no longer find ourselves in the framework of classic tonality in the scholastic sense of the word. It is not we who have created this state of affairs, and it is not our fault if we find ourselves confronted with a new logic of music that would have appeared unthinkable to the masters of the past. And this new logic has opened our eyes to riches whose existence we never suspected.

Having reached this point, it is no less indispensable to obey, not new idols, but the eternal necessity of affirming the axis of our music and to recognize the existence of certain poles of attraction. Diatonic tonality is only one means of orienting music towards these poles. The function of tonality is completely subordinated to the force of attraction of the pole of sonority. All music is nothing more than a succession of impulses that converge towards a definite point of repose. That is as true of Gregorian chant as it is of a

Bach fugue, as true of Brahms's music as it is of Debussy's.

This general law of attraction is satisfied in only a limited way by the traditional diatonic system, for that system possesses no absolute value.

There are few present-day musicians who are not aware of this state of affairs. But the fact remains that it is still impossible to lay down the rules that govern this new technique. Nor is this at all surprising. Harmony as it is taught today in the schools dictates rules that were not fixed until long after the publication of the works upon which they were based, rules which were unknown to the composers of these works. In this manner our harmonic treatises take as their point of departure Mozart and Haydn, neither of whom ever heard of harmonic treatises.

So our chief concern is not so much what is known as tonality as what one might term the polar attraction of sound, of an interval, or even of a complex of tones. The sounding tone constitutes in a way the essential axis of music. Musical form would be unimaginable in the absence of elements of attraction which make up every musical organism and which are bound up with its psychology. The articulations of musical discourse betray a hidden correlation between the *tempo* and the interplay of tones. All music being nothing but a succession of impulses and repose, it is easy to see that the drawing together and separation of poles of attraction in a way determine the respiration of music.

In view of the fact that our poles of attraction are no longer within the closed system which was the diatonic system, we can bring the poles together without being compelled to conform to the exigencies of tonality. For we no longer believe in the absolute value of the major-minor system based on the entity which musicologists call the c-scale.

The tuning of an instrument, of a piano for example, requires that the entire musical range available to the instrument should be ordered according to chromatic steps. Such tuning prompts us to observe that all these sounds converge towards a center which is the a above middle c. Composing, for me, is putting into an order a certain number of these sounds according to certain interval-relationships. This activity leads to a search for the center upon which the series of sounds involved in my undertaking should converge. Thus, if a center is given, I shall have to find a combination that converges upon it. If, on the other hand, an as yet unoriented combination has been found, I shall have to determine the center towards which it should lead. The discovery of this center suggests to me the solution of my problem. It is thus that I satisfy my very marked taste for such a kind of musical topography.

The superannuated system of classic tonality, which has served as the basis for musical constructions of compelling interest, has had the authority of law among musicians for only a short period of time — a period much shorter than is usually imagined, extending only from the middle of the seventeenth century to the middle of the nineteenth. From the moment when chords no longer serve to fulfill merely the functions assigned to them by the interplay of tones but, instead, throw off all constraint to become new entities free of all ties — from that moment on one may say that the process is completed: the diatonic system has lived out its life cycle. The work of the Renaissance polyphonists had not yet entered into this system, and we have seen that the music of our time abides by it no longer. A parallel progression of ninth-chords would suffice as proof. It was here that the gates opened upon what has been labeled with the abusive term: *atonality*.

The expression is fashionable. But that doesn't mean that it is very clear. And I should like to know just what those persons who use the term mean by it. The negating prefix *a* indicates a state of indifference in regard to the term, negating without entirely renouncing it. Understood in this way, the word *atonality* hardly corresponds to what those who use it have in mind. If it were said that my music is atonal, that would be tantamount to saying that I had become deaf to tonality. Now it well may be that I remain for a considerable time within the bounds of the strict order of tonality, even though I may quite consciously break up this order for the purposes of establishing a new one. In that case I am not *a*tonal, but *anti*tonal. I am not trying to argue pointlessly over words: it is essential to know what we deny and what we affirm.

Modality, tonality, polarity are merely provisional

38

means that are passing by, and will even pass away. What survives every change of system is melody. The masters of the Middle Ages and of the Renaissance were no less concerned over melody than were Bach and Mozart. But my musical topography does not reserve a place for melody alone. It reserves for melody the same position that devolved upon it under the modal and diatonic systems.

We know that the term melody, in the scientific meaning of the word, is applied to the top voice in polyphony, thus differentiating melody from the unaccompanied cantilena that is called *monody*.

Melody, *Mélôdia* in Greek, is the intonation of the *melos*, which signifies a fragment, a part of a phrase. It is these parts that strike the ear in such a way as to mark certain accentuations. Melody is thus the musical singing of a cadenced phrase — I use the word *cadenced* in its general sense, not in the special musical sense. The capacity for melody is a gift. This means that it is not within our power to develop it by study. But at least we can regulate its evolution by perspicacious self-criticism. The example of Beethoven would suffice to convince us that, of all the elements of music, melody is the most accessible to the ear and the least capable of acquisition. Here we have one of the greatest creators of music who spent his whole life imploring the aid of this gift which he lacked. So that this admirable deaf man developed his extraordinary faculties in direct proportion to the resistance offered him by the one he lacked, just the way a blind man in his eternal night develops the sharpness of his auditive sense.

The Germans, as we all know, honor their four great B's. On a more modest plane we shall select two B's for the needs of our argument.

At the time when Beethoven bequeathed to the world riches partly attributable to the recalcitrance of the melodic gift, another composer, whose achievements were never equal to those of the master of Bonn, scattered to the winds with indefatigable profusion magnificent melodies of the rarest quality, distributing them as gratuitously as he had received them, without even being aware of the merit of having created them. Beethoven amassed a patrimony for music that seems to be solely the result of obstinate labor. Bellini inherited melody without having even so much as asked for it, as if Heaven had said to him, "I shall give you the one thing Beethoven lacks."

Under the influence of the learned intellectualism that held sway among music-lovers of the serious sort, it was for a time fashionable to disdain melody. I am beginning to think, in full agreement with the general public, that melody must keep its place at the summit of the hierarchy of elements that make up music. Melody is the most essential of these elements, not because it is more immediately perceptible, but because it is the dominant voice of the symphony — not only in the specific sense, but also figuratively speaking.

But that is no reason for allowing ourselves to be beclouded by melody to the point of losing balance and of forgetting that the art of music speaks to us in many voices at once. Let me once again call your attention to Beethoven, whose greatness derives from a stubborn battle with rebellious melody. If melody were all of music, what could we prize in the various forces that make up the immense work of Beethoven, in which melody is assuredly the least?

If it is easy to define melody, it is much less easy to distinguish the characteristics that make a melody beautiful. The appraisal of a value is itself subject to appraisal. The only standard we possess in these matters depends on a fineness of culture that presupposes the perfection of taste. Nothing here is absolute except the relative.

A system of tonal or polar centers is given to us solely for the purpose of achieving a certain order, that is to say more definitively, form, the form in which the creative effort culminates.

Of all musical forms, the one considered the richest from the point of view of development is the symphony. We usually designate by that name a composition in several movements, of which one confers upon the whole work its symphonic quality — namely, the symphonic *allegro*, generally placed at the opening of the work and intended to justify its name by fulfilling the requirements of a certain musical dialectic. The essential part of this dialectic resides in the central portion, the development. It is precisely this symphonic allegro, which is also termed the sonata-allegro, that determines the form upon which, as we know, all instrumental music is constructed — from the sonata for a solo instrument through the various chamber ensembles (trios, quartets, and so on) all the way to the most extensive compositions for huge orchestral masses. But I do not wish to bother you further with a course in morphology that does not correspond exactly to the object of my lessons, and I only mention the subject in passing to remind you that there exists in music, just as in all the other arts, a sort of hierarchy of forms.

It is customary to distinguish instrumental forms from vocal forms. The instrumental element enjoys an autonomy that the vocal element does not enjoy, since the latter is bound to words. Through the course of history each of these media has left its impress upon the forms to which it has given rise. Basically, such distinctions constitute only artificial categories. Form is born of the tonal medium, but each medium so readily borrows forms that were developed by other media that the mingling of styles is constant and makes discrimination impossible.

Great centers of culture, such as the Church, have in the past welcomed and cultivated vocal art. In our time choral societies can no longer fulfill the same task. Reduced to upholding and presenting the works of the past, they cannot lay claim to playing the same role, because the evolution of vocal polyphony has been arrested for a long time. Song, more and more bound to words, has finally become a sort of filler, thereby evidencing its decadence. From the moment song assumes as its calling the expression of the meaning of discourse, it leaves the realm of music and has nothing more in common with it.

Nothing shows more clearly the power of Wagner and of the kind of storm and stress which he unleashed than this decadence which his work actually consecrated and that has developed apace ever since his time. How powerful this man must have been to have destroyed an essentially musical form with such energy that fifty years after his death we are still staggering under the rubbish and racket of the music drama! For the prestige of the *Synthesis of the Arts* is still alive.

Is that what is called progress? Perhaps. Unless composers find the strength to shake off this heavy legacy by obeying Verdi's admirable injunction: "Let us return to old times, and that will be progress."

3. THE COMPOSITION OF MUSIC

E ARE LIVING AT A
time when the status of man is undergoing profound
upheavals. Modern man is progressively losing his
understanding of values and his sense of proportions.
This failure to understand essential realities is extremely serious. It leads us infallibly to the violation
of the fundamental laws of human equilibrium. In the
domain of music, the consequences of this misunderstanding are these: on one hand there is a tendency to
turn the mind away from what I shall call the higher
mathematics of music in order to degrade music to
servile employment, and to vulgarize it by adapting it
to the requirements of an elementary utilitarianism —
as we shall soon see on examining Soviet music. On
the other hand, since the mind itself is ailing, the
music of our time, and particularly the music that calls
itself and believes itself *pure*, carries within it the
symptoms of a pathologic blemish and spreads the
germs of a new original sin. The old original sin was
chiefly a sin of knowledge; the new original sin, if I
may speak in these terms, is first and foremost a sin of
non-acknowledgement — a refusal to acknowledge the

47

truth and the laws that proceed therefrom, laws that we have called fundamental. What then is this truth in the domain of music? And what are its repercussions on creative activity?

Let us not forget that it is written: "Spiritus ubi vult spirat" (St. John, 3: 8). What we must retain in this proposition is above all the word WILL. The Spirit is thus endowed with the capacity of willing. The principle of speculative volition is a fact.

Now it is just this fact that is too often disputed. People question the direction that the wind of the Spirit is taking, not the rightness of the artisan's work. In so doing, whatever may be your feelings about ontology or whatever your own philosophy and beliefs may be, you must admit that you are making an attack on the very freedom of the spirit — whether you begin this large word with a capital or not. If a believer in Christian philosophy, you would then also have to refuse to accept the idea of the Holy Spirit. If an agnostic or atheist, you would have to do nothing less than refuse to be a *free-thinker* . . .

It should be noted that there is never any dispute when the listener takes pleasure in the work he hears. The least informed of music-lovers readily clings to the periphery of a work; it pleases him for reasons that are most often entirely foreign to the essence of music. This pleasure is enough for him and calls for no justification. But if it happens that the music displeases him, our music-lover will ask you for an explanation of his discomfiture. He will demand that we explain something that is in its essence ineffable.

By its fruit we judge the tree. Judge the tree by its fruit then, and do not meddle with the roots. Function justifies an organ, no matter how strange the organ may appear in the eyes of those who are not accustomed to see it functioning. Snobbish circles are cluttered with persons who, like one of Montesquieu's characters, wonder how one can possibly be a Persian. They make me think unfailingly of the story of the peasant who, on seeing a dromedary in the zoo for the first time, examines it at length, shakes his head and, turning to leave, says, to the great delight of those present: "It isn't true."

It is through the unhampered play of its functions, then, that a work is revealed and justified. We are free to accept or reject this play, but no one has the right to question the fact of its existence. To judge, dispute, and criticize the principle of speculative volition which is at the origin of all creation is thus manifestly useless. In the pure state, music is free speculation. Artists of all epochs have unceasingly testified to this concept. For myself, I see no reason for not trying to do as they did. Since I myself was created, I cannot help having the desire to create. What sets this desire in motion, and what can I do to make it productive?

The study of the creative process is an extremely delicate one. In truth, it is impossible to observe the inner workings of this process from the outside. It is futile to try and follow its successive phases in someone else's work. It is likewise very difficult to observe one's self. Yet it is only by enlisting the aid of introspection that I may have any chance at all of guiding you in this essentially fluctuating matter.

Most music-lovers believe that what sets the composer's creative imagination in motion is a certain emotive disturbance generally designated by the name of *inspiration*.

I have no thought of denying to inspiration the outstanding role that has devolved upon it in the generative process we are studying; I simply maintain that inspiration is in no way a prescribed condition of the creative act, but rather a manifestation that is chronologically secondary.

Inspiration, art, artist — so many words, hazy at least, that keep us from seeing clearly in a field where everything is balance and calculation through which the breath of the speculative spirit blows. It is afterwards, and only afterwards, that the emotive disturbance which is at the root of inspiration may arise — an emotive disturbance about which people talk so indelicately by conferring upon it a meaning that is shocking to us and that compromises the term itself. Is it not clear that this emotion is merely a reaction on the part of the creator grappling with that unknown entity which is still only the object of his creating and which is to become a work of art? Step by step, link by link, it will be granted him to discover the work. It is this chain of discoveries, as well as each individual discovery, that give rise to the emotion — an almost physiological reflex, like that of the appetite causing a flow of saliva — this emotion which invariably follows closely the phases of the creative process.

All creation presupposes at its origin a sort of appetite that is brought on by the foretaste of discovery. This foretaste of the creative act accompanies the intuitive grasp of an unknown entity already possessed but not yet intelligible, an entity that will not take definite shape except by the action of a constantly vigilant technique.

This appetite that is aroused in me at the mere thought of putting in order musical elements that have attracted my attention is not at all a fortuitous thing like inspiration, but as habitual and periodic, if not as constant, as a natural need.

This premonition of an obligation, this foretaste of a pleasure, this conditioned reflex, as a modern physiologist would say, shows clearly that it is the idea of discovery and hard work that attracts me.

The very act of putting my work on paper, of, as we say, kneading the dough, is for me inseparable from the pleasure of creation. So far as I am concerned, I cannot separate the spiritual effort from the psychological and physical effort; they confront me on the same level and do not present a hierarchy.

The word *artist* which, as it is most generally understood today, bestows on its bearer the highest intellectual prestige, the privilege of being accepted as a pure mind — this pretentious term is in my view entirely incompatible with the role of the *homo faber*.

At this point it should be remembered that, whatever field of endeavor has fallen to our lot, if it is true that we are *intellectuals*, we are called upon not to cogitate, but to perform.

The philosopher Jacques Maritain reminds us that in the mighty structure of medieval civilization, the artist held only the rank of an artisan. "And his individualism was forbidden any sort of anarchic development, because a natural social discipline imposed certain limitative conditions upon him from without." It was the Renaissance that invented the artist, distinguished him from the artisan and began to exalt the former at the expense of the latter.

At the outset the name artist was given only to the Masters of Arts: philosophers, alchemists, magicians; but painters, sculptors, musicians, and poets had the right to be qualified only as artisans.

> Plying divers implements,
> The subtile artizan implants
> Life in marble, copper, bronze,

says the poet Du Bellay. And Montaigne enumerates in his *Essays* the "painters, poets and other artizans." And even in the seventeenth century, La Fontaine hails a painter with the name of *artisan* and draws a sharp rebuke from an ill-tempered critic who might have been the ancestor of most of our present-day critics.

The idea of work to be done is for me so closely bound up with the idea of the arranging of materials and of the pleasure that the actual doing of the work affords us that, should the impossible happen and my work suddenly be given to me in a perfectly completed form, I should be embarrassed and nonplussed by it, as by a hoax.

We have a duty towards music, namely, to invent it. I recall once during the war when I was crossing the French border a gendarme asked me what my profession was. I told him quite naturally that I was an inventor of music. The gendarme, then verifying my passport, asked me why I was listed as a composer. I told him that the expression "inventor of music" seemed to me to fit my profession more exactly than the term applied to me in the documents authorizing me to cross borders.

Invention presupposes imagination but should not be confused with it. For the act of invention implies the necessity of a lucky find and of achieving full realization of this find. What we imagine does not necessarily take on a concrete form and may remain in a state of virtuality, whereas invention is not conceivable apart from its actual being worked out.

Thus, what concerns us here is not imagination in itself, but rather creative imagination: the faculty that helps us to pass from the level of conception to the level of realization.

In the course of my labors I suddenly stumble upon something unexpected. This unexpected element strikes me. I make a note of it. At the proper time I put it to profitable use. This gift of chance must not be confused with that capriciousness of imagination that is commonly called fancy. Fancy implies a predetermined will to abandon one's self to caprice. The aforementioned assistance of the unexpected is something quite different. It is a collaboration which is immanently bound up with the inertia of the creative process and is heavy with possibilities which are unsolicited and come most appositely to temper the inevitable over-rigorousness of the naked will. And it is good that this is so.

"In everything that yields gracefully," G. K. Chesterton says somewhere, "there must be resistance. Bows are beautiful when they bend only because they seek to remain rigid. Rigidity that slightly yields, like Justice swayed by Pity, is all the beauty of earth. Everything seeks to grow straight, and happily, nothing succeeds in so growing. Try to grow straight and life will bend you."

The faculty of creating is never given to us all by itself. It always goes hand in hand with the gift of observation. And the true creator may be recognized by his ability always to find about him, in the commonest and humblest thing, items worthy of note. He does not have to concern himself with a beautiful landscape, he does not need to surround himself with rare and precious objects. He does not have to put forth in search of discoveries: they are always within his reach. He will have only to cast a glance about him. Familiar things, things that are everywhere, attract his attention. The least accident holds his interest and guides his operations. If his finger slips, he will notice it; on occasion, he may draw profit from something unforeseen that a momentary lapse reveals to him.

One does not contrive an accident: one observes it to draw inspiration therefrom. An accident is perhaps the only thing that really inspires us. A composer improvises aimlessly the way an animal grubs about. Both of them go grubbing about because they yield to a compulsion to seek things out. What urge of the composer is satisfied by this investigation? The rules with which, like a penitent, he is burdened? No: he is in quest of his pleasure. He seeks a satisfaction that he fully knows he will not find without first striving for it. One cannot force one's self to love; but love presupposes understanding, and in order to understand, one must exert one's self.

It is the same problem that was posed in the Middle Ages by the theologians of pure love. To understand in order to love; to love in order to understand: we are here not going around in a vicious circle; we are rising spirally, providing we have made an initial effort, have even just gone through a routine exercise.

Pascal has specifically this in mind when he writes that custom "controls the automaton, which in its turn unthinkingly controls the mind. For there must be no mistake," continues Pascal, "we are automatons just as much as we are minds . . ."

So we grub about in expectation of our pleasure, guided by our scent, and suddenly we stumble against an unknown obstacle. It gives us a jolt, a shock, and this shock fecundates our creative power.

The faculty of observation and of making something out of what is observed belongs only to the person who at least possesses, in his particular field of endeavor, an acquired culture and an innate taste. A dealer, an art-lover who is the first to buy the canvases of an unknown painter who will be famous twenty-five years later under the name of Cézanne — doesn't such a person give us a clear example of this innate taste? What else guides him in his choice? A flair, an instinct from which this taste proceeds, a completely spontaneous faculty anterior to reflection.

As for culture, it is a sort of upbringing which, in the social sphere, confers polish upon education, sustains and rounds out academic instruction. This upbringing is just as important in the sphere of taste and is essential to the creator who must ceaselessly refine his taste or run the risk of losing his perspicacity. Our mind, as well as our body, requires continual exercise. It atrophies if we do not cultivate it.

It is culture that brings out the full value of taste and gives it a chance to prove its worth simply by its application. The artist imposes a culture upon himself and ends by imposing it upon others. That is how tradition becomes established.

Tradition is entirely different from habit, even from an excellent habit, since habit is by definition an unconscious acquisition and tends to become mechanical, whereas tradition results from a conscious and deliberate acceptance. A real tradition is not the relic of a past that is irretrievably gone; it is a living force that animates and informs the present. In this sense the paradox which banteringly maintains that everything which is not tradition is plagiarism, is true . . .

Far from implying the repetition of what has been, tradition presupposes the reality of what endures. It appears as an heirloom, a heritage that one receives on condition of making it bear fruit before passing it on to one's descendants.

Brahms was born sixty years after Beethoven. From the one to the other, and from every aspect, the distance is great; they do not dress the same way, but Brahms follows the tradition of Beethoven without borrowing one of his habiliments. For the borrowing of a method has nothing to do with observing a tradition. "A method is replaced: a tradition is carried forward in order to produce something new." Tradition thus assures the continuity of creation. The example that I have just cited does not constitute an exception but is one proof out of a hundred of a constant law. This sense of tradition which is a natural need must not be confused with the desire which the composer feels to affirm the kinship he finds across the centuries with some master of the past.

My opera *Mavra* was born of a natural sympathy for the body of melodic tendencies, for the vocal style and conventional language which I came to admire more and more in the old Russo-Italian opera. This sympathy guided me quite naturally along the path of a tradition that seemed to be lost at the moment when the attention of musical circles was turned entirely towards the music drama, which represented no tradition at all from the historical point of view and which fulfilled no necessity at all from the musical point of view. The vogue of the music drama had a pathological origin. Alas, even the admirable music of *Pélléas et Mélisande*, so fresh in its modesty, was unable to get us into the open, in spite of so many characteristics with which it shook off the tyranny of the Wagnerian system.

The music of *Mavra* stays within the tradition of Glinka and Dargomisky. I had not the slightest intention of reëstablishing this tradition. I simply wanted in my turn to try my hand at the living form of the *opéra-bouffe* which was so well suited to the Pushkin tale which gave me my subject. *Mavra* is dedicated to the memory of composers, not one of whom, I am sure, would have recognized as valid such a manifestation of the tradition they created, because of the novelty of the language my music speaks a hundred years after its models flourished. But I wanted to renew the style of these dialogues-in-music whose voices had been reviled and drowned out by the clang and clatter of the music drama. So a hundred years had to pass before the freshness of the Russo-Italian tradition could again be appreciated, a tradition that continued to live apart from the main stream of the present, and in which circulated a salubrious air, well adapted to delivering us from the miasmic vapors of the music drama, the inflated arrogance of which could not conceal its vacuity.

I am not without motive in provoking a quarrel with the notorious Synthesis of the Arts. I do not merely condemn it for its lack of tradition, its *nouveau riche* smugness. What makes its case much worse is the fact that the application of its theories has inflicted a terrible blow upon music itself. In every period of spiritual anarchy wherein man, having lost his feeling and taste for ontology, takes fright at himself and at his destiny, there always appears one of these gnosticisms which serve as a religion for those who no longer have a religion, just as in periods of international crises an army of soothsayers, fakirs, and clairvoyants monopolize journalistic publicity. We can speak of these things all the more freely in view of the fact that the halcyon days of Wagnerism are past and that the distance which separates us from them permits us to set matters straight again. Sound minds, moreover, never believed in the paradise of the Synthesis of the Arts and have always recognized its enchantments at their true worth.

I have said that I never saw any necessity for music to adopt such a dramatic system. I shall add something more: I hold that this system, far from having raised the level of musical culture, has never ceased to undermine it and finally to debase it in the most paradoxical fashion. In the past one went to the opera for the diversion offered by facile musical works. Later on one returned to it in order to yawn at dramas in which music, arbitrarily paralyzed by constraints for-

59

eign to its own laws, could not help tiring out the most attentive audience in spite of the great talent displayed by Wagner.

So, from music shamelessly considered as a purely sensual delight, we passed without transition to the murky inanities of the Art-Religion, with its heroic hardware, its arsenal of warrior-mysticism and its vocabulary seasoned with an adulterated religiosity. So that as soon as music ceased to be scorned, it was only to find itself smothered under literary flowers. It succeeded in getting a hearing from the cultured public thanks only to a misunderstanding which tended to turn drama into a hodgepodge of symbols, and music itself into an object of philosophical speculation. That is how the speculative spirit came to lose its course and how it came to betray music while ostensibly trying to serve it the better.

Music based upon the opposite principles has, unfortunately, not yet given proofs of its worth in our own period. It is curious to note that it was a musician who proclaimed himself a Wagnerian, the Frenchman Chabrier, who was able to maintain the sound tradition of dramatic art in those difficult times and who excelled in the French *opéra comique* along with a few of his compatriots, at the very height of the Wagnerian vogue. Is not this the tradition that is continued in the sparkling group of masterpieces that are called *Le Médecin malgré lui, La Colombe, Philémon et Baucis* of Gounod; *Lakmé, Coppélia, Sylvia* of Léo Delibes; *Carmen* by Bizet; *Le Roi malgré lui, L'Etoile*

60

of Chabrier; *La Béarnaise, Véronique* of Messager —
to which has just recently been added the *Chartreuse
de Parme* by the young Henri Sauguet?

Think how subtle and clinging the poison of the
music drama was to have insinuated itself even into
the veins of the colossus Verdi.

How can we help regretting that this master of the
traditional opera, at the end of a long life studded with
so many authentic masterpieces, climaxed his career
with *Falstaff* which, if it is not Wagner's best work, is
not Verdi's best opera either?

I know that I am going counter to the general opinion that sees Verdi's best work in the deterioration of
the genius that gave us *Rigoletto, Il Trovatore, Aïda,*
and *La Traviata.* I know I am defending precisely
what the elite of the recent past belittled in the works
of this great composer. I regret having to say so;
but I maintain that there is more substance and true
invention in the aria *La donna è mobile*, for example, in which this elite saw nothing but deplorable
facility, than in the rhetoric and vociferations of the
Ring.

Whether we admit it or not, the Wagnerian drama
reveals continual bombast. Its brilliant improvisations
inflate the symphony beyond all proportion and give
it less real substance than the invention, at once modest and aristocratic, that blossoms forth on every page
of Verdi.

At the beginning of my course I gave notice that I
would continually come back to the necessity for order

and discipline; and here I must weary you again by returning to the same theme.

Richard Wagner's music is more improvised than constructed, in the specific musical sense. Arias, ensembles, and their reciprocal relationships in the structure of an opera confer upon the whole work a coherence that is merely the external and visible manifestation of an internal and profound order.

The antagonism of Wagner and Verdi very neatly illustrates my thoughts on this subject.

While Verdi was being relegated to the organ-grinder's repertory, it was fashionable to hail in Wagner the typical revolutionary. Nothing is more significant than this relegation of order to the muse of the street corners at the moment when one found sublimity in the cult of disorder.

Wagner's work corresponds to a tendency that is not, properly speaking, a disorder, but one which tries to compensate for a lack of order. The principle of the endless melody perfectly illustrates this tendency. It is the perpetual becoming of a music that never had any reason for starting, any more than it has any reason for ending. Endless melody thus appears as an insult to the dignity and to the very function of melody which, as we have said, is the musical intonation of a cadenced phrase. Under the influence of Wagner the laws that secure the life of song found themselves violated, and music lost its melodic smile. Perhaps his method of doing things answered a need; but this need was not compatible with the possibilities of musical art, for musical art is limited in its expression in a measure corresponding exactly to the limitations of the organ that perceives it. A mode of composition that does not assign itself limits becomes pure fantasy. The effects it produces may accidentally amuse but are not capable of being repeated. I cannot conceive of a fantasy that is repeated, for it can be repeated only to its detriment.

Let us understand each other in regard to this word fantasy. We are not using the word in the sense in which it is connected with a definite musical form, but in the acceptation which presupposes an abandonment of one's self to the caprices of imagination. And this presupposes that the composer's will is voluntarily paralyzed. For imagination is not only the mother of caprice but the servant and handmaiden of the creative will as well.

The creator's function is to sift the elements he receives from her, for human activity must impose limits upon itself. The more art is controlled, limited, worked over, the more it is free.

As for myself, I experience a sort of terror when, at the moment of setting to work and finding myself before the infinitude of possibilities that present themselves, I have the feeling that everything is permissible to me. If everything is permissible to me, the best and the worst; if nothing offers me any resistance, then any effort is inconceivable, and I cannot use anything as a basis, and consequently every undertaking becomes futile.

63

Will I then have to lose myself in this abyss of freedom? To what shall I cling in order to escape the dizziness that seizes me before the virtuality of this infinitude? However, I shall not succumb. I shall overcome my terror and shall be reassured by the thought that I have the seven notes of the scale and its chromatic intervals at my disposal, that strong and weak accents are within my reach, and that in all of these I possess solid and concrete elements which offer me a field of experience just as vast as the upsetting and dizzy infinitude that had just frightened me. It is into this field that I shall sink my roots, fully convinced that combinations which have at their disposal twelve sounds in each octave and all possible rhythmic varieties promise me riches that all the activity of human genius will never exhaust.

What delivers me from the anguish into which an unrestricted freedom plunges me is the fact that I am always able to turn immediately to the concrete things that are here in question. I have no use for a theoretic freedom. Let me have something finite, definite — matter that can lend itself to my operation only insofar as it is commensurate with my possibilities. And such matter presents itself to me together with its limitations. I must in turn impose mine upon it. So here we are, whether we like it or not, in the realm of necessity. And yet which of us has ever heard talk of art as other than a realm of freedom? This sort of heresy is uniformly widespread because it is imagined that art is outside the bounds of ordinary activity. Well, in art as in everything else, one can build only upon a resisting foundation: whatever constantly gives way to pressure, constantly renders movement impossible.

My freedom thus consists in my moving about within the narrow frame that I have assigned myself for each one of my undertakings.

I shall go even further: my freedom will be so much the greater and more meaningful the more narrowly I limit my field of action and the more I surround myself with obstacles. Whatever diminishes constraint, diminishes strength. The more constraints one imposes, the more one frees one's self of the chains that shackle the spirit.

To the voice that commands me to create I first respond with fright; then I reassure myself by taking up as weapons those things participating in creation but as yet outside of it; and the arbitrariness of the constraint serves only to obtain precision of execution.

From all this we shall conclude the necessity of dogmatizing on pain of missing our goal. If these words annoy us and seem harsh, we can abstain from pronouncing them. For all that, they nonetheless contain the secret of salvation: "It is evident," writes Baudelaire, "that rhetorics and prosodies are not arbitrarily invented tyrannies, but a collection of rules demanded by the very organization of the spiritual being, and never have prosodies and rhetorics kept originality from fully manifesting itself. The contrary, that is to say, that they have aided the flowering of originality, would be infinitely more true."

4. MUSICAL TYPOLOGY

LL ART PRESUPPOSES A
work of selection. Usually when I set to work my goal
is not definite. If I were asked what I wanted at this
stage of the creative process, I should be hard pressed
to say. But I should always give an exact answer when
asked what I did *not* want.

To proceed by elimination — to know how to *dis-
card*, as the gambler says, that is the great technique
of selection. And here again we find the search for the
One out of the *Many* to which we referred in our second lesson.

I should find it very hard to show in what way this
principle is embodied in my music. I shall try to con-
vey it to you rather by setting forth my general tendencies than by citing particular facts as examples: if
I proceed by the juxtaposition of strongly clashing
tones, I can produce an immediate and violent sensation. If, on the other hand, I contrive to bring together
closely related colors, I attain my goal less directly but
more surely. The principle of this method reveals the
subconscious activity that makes us incline towards
unity; for we instinctively prefer coherence and its

quiet strength to the restless powers of dispersion —
that is, we prefer the realm of order to the realm of
dissimilarity.

Since my own experience shows me the necessity of
discarding in order to select and the necessity of differentiating in order to unite, it seems to me that by extension I can apply this principle to the whole of
music, thereby to establish a picture in perspective, a
stereoscopic view of the history of my art and also to
see what constitutes the real physiognomy of a composer or of a school.

This will be our contribution to the study of musical
types — to typology — and to an examination of the
problem of style.

Style is the particular way a composer organizes his
conceptions and speaks the language of his craft. This
musical language is the element common to the composers of a particular school or epoch. Certainly the
musical physiognomies of Mozart and Haydn are well
known to you, and certainly you have not failed to notice that these composers are obviously related to each
other, although it is easy for those who are familiar
with the language of the period to distinguish them.

The attire that fashion prescribes for men of the
same generation imposes upon its wearers a particular
kind of gesture, a common carriage and bearing, that
are conditioned by the cut of the clothes. In a like
manner the musical apparel worn by an epoch leaves
its stamp upon the language, and, so to speak, upon
the gestures of its music, as well as upon the compos-

70

er's attitude towards tonal materials. These elements are the immediate factors of the mass of particulars that help us to determine how musical language and style are formed.

There is no need to tell you that what is called the style of an epoch results from a combination of individual styles, a combination which is dominated by the methods of the composers who have exerted a preponderant influence on their time.

We can notice, going back to the example of Mozart and Haydn, that they benefited from the same culture, drew on the same sources, and borrowed each other's discoveries. Each of them, however, works a miracle all his own.

One may say that the masters, who in all their greatness surpass the generality of their contemporaries, send out the rays of their genius well beyond their own day. In this way they appear as powerful signal-fires — as beacons, to use Baudelaire's expression — by whose light and warmth is developed a sum of tendencies that will be shared by most of their successors and that contributes to form the parcel of traditions which make up a culture.

These great beacon-fires which shine out at widely separated distances upon the historical field of art promote the continuity that gives the true and only legitimate meaning to a much abused word, to that evolution which has been revered as a goddess — a goddess who turned out to be somewhat of a tramp, let it be said in passing, even to having given birth to a little bastard myth that looks very much like her and that has been named Progress, with a capital P . . .

For the devotees of the religion of Progress, today is always and necessarily more worth while than yesterday, from which the consequence necessarily follows that in the field of music the opulent contemporary orchestra represents an advance over the modest instrumental ensembles of former times — that the Wagnerian orchestra represents an advance over that of Beethoven. I leave it to you to judge what such a preference is worth . . .

The beautiful continuity that makes possible the development of culture appears as a general rule that suffers a few exceptions which, one might say, were expressly created to confirm it.

In fact, at widely separated intervals one sees an erratic block silhouetted on the horizon of art, a block whose origin is unknown and whose existence is incomprehensible. These monoliths seem heaven-sent to affirm the existence, and in a certain measure the legitimacy, of the accidental. These elements of discontinuity, these sports of nature bear various names in our art. The most curious is named Hector Berlioz. His prestige is great. It can be attributed above all to the *brio* of an orchestra that evidences the most disquieting originality, an originality entirely gratuitous, without foundation, one that is insufficient to disguise the poverty of invention. And if it is maintained that Berlioz is one of the originators of the tone poem, I shall answer that that type of composition — which was, by the way, very short-lived — cannot be considered on the same footing as the great symphonic forms, since it seeks to be entirely dependent on elements foreign to music. In this respect Berlioz's influence is greater in the field of aesthetics than in music; when this influence makes itself felt in Liszt, Balakirev, and the Rimski-Korsakov of the youthful works, it leaves the core of their music untouched.

The great beacon-fires we spoke about never flare up without causing profound disturbances in the world of music. Afterwards things become stabilized again. The fire's radiation becomes more and more attenuated until the moment comes when it warms none but the pedagogues. At that point academicism is born. But a new beacon-fire appears, and the story goes on — which does not mean that it goes on without shock or accident. It just so happens that our contemporary epoch offers us the example of a musical culture that is day by day losing the sense of continuity and the taste for a common language.

Individual caprice and intellectual anarchy, which tend to control the world in which we live, isolate the artist from his fellow-artists and condemn him to appear as a monster in the eyes of the public; a monster of originality, inventor of his own language, of his own vocabulary, and of the apparatus of his art. The use of already employed materials and of established forms is usually forbidden him. So he comes to the point of speaking an idiom without relation to the world that listens to him. His art becomes truly

73

unique, in the sense that it is incommunicable and shut off on every side. The erratic block is no longer a curiosity that is an exception; it is the sole model offered neophytes for emulation.

The appearance of a series of anarchic, incompatible, and contradictory tendencies in the field of history corresponds to this complete break in tradition. Times have changed since the day when Bach, Handel, and Vivaldi quite evidently spoke the same language which their disciples repeated after them, each one unwittingly transforming this language according to his own personality. The day when Haydn, Mozart, and Cimarosa echoed each other in works that served their successors as models, successors such as Rossini, who was fond of repeating in so touching a way that Mozart had been the delight of his youth, the desperation of his maturity, and the consolation of his old age.

Those times have given way to a new age that seeks to reduce everything to uniformity in the realm of matter while it tends to shatter all universality in the realm of the spirit in deference to an anarchic individualism. That is how once universal centers of culture have become isolated. They withdraw into a national, even regional, framework which in its turn splits up to the point of eventual disappearance.

Whether he wills it or not, the contemporary artist is caught in this infernal machination. There are simple souls who rejoice in this state of affairs. There are criminals who approve of it. Only a few are horrified at a solitude that obliges them to turn in upon themselves when everything invites them to participate in social life.

The universality whose benefits we are gradually losing is an entirely different thing from the cosmopolitanism that is beginning to take hold of us. Universality presupposes the fecundity of a culture that is spread and communicated everywhere, whereas cosmopolitanism provides for neither action nor doctrine and induces the indifferent passivity of a sterile eclecticism.

Universality necessarily stipulates submission to an established order. And its reasons for this stipulation are convincing. We submit to this order out of sympathy or prudence. In either case the benefits of submission are not long in appearing.

In a society like that of the Middle Ages, which recognized and safeguarded the primacy of the spiritual realm and the dignity of the human person (which must not be confused with the individual) — in such a society recognition by everyone of a hierarchy of values and a body of moral principles established an order of things that put everyone in accord concerning certain fundamental concepts of good and evil, truth and error. I do not say of beauty and ugliness, because it is absolutely futile to dogmatize in so subjective a domain.

It should not surprise us then that social order has never directly governed these matters. As a matter of fact, it is not by promulgating an aesthetic but by improving the status of man and by exalting the competent workman in the artist that a civilization communicates something of its order to works of art and speculation. The good artisan himself in those happy ages dreams of achieving the *beautiful* only through the categories of the *useful*. His prime concern is applied to the rightness of an operation that is performed *well*, in keeping with a *true* order. The aesthetic impression that will arise from this rightness will not be legitimately achieved except insofar as it was not calculated. Poussin said quite correctly that "the goal of art is delectation." He did not say that this delectation should be the goal of the artist who must always submit solely to the demands of the work to be done.

It is a fact of experience, and one that is only seemingly paradoxical, that we find freedom in a strict submission to the object: "It is not wisdom, but foolishness, that is stubborn," says Sophocles, in the magnificent translation of *Antigone* given us by André Bonnard. "Look at the trees. By embracing the movements of the tempest they preserve their tender branches; but if they rear against the wind they are carried off, roots and all."

Let us take the best example: the fugue, a pure form in which the music means nothing outside itself. Doesn't the fugue imply the composer's submission to the rules? And is it not within those strictures that he finds the full flowering of his freedom as a creator? Strength, says Leonardo da Vinci, is born of constraint and dies in freedom.

Insubordination boasts of just the opposite and does

away with constraint in the ever-disappointed hope of finding in freedom the principle of strength. Instead, it finds in freedom only the arbitrariness of whim and the disorders of fancy. Thus it loses every vestige of control, loses its bearings and ends by demanding of music things which are outside its scope and competence. Do we not, in truth, ask the impossible of music when we expect it to express feelings, to translate dramatic situations, even to imitate nature? And, as if it were not enough to condemn music to the job of being an illustrator, the century to which we owe what it called "progress through enlightenment" invented for good measure the monumental absurdity which consists of bestowing on every accessory, as well as on every feeling and every character of the lyrical drama, a sort of check-room number called a *Leitmotiv* — a system that led Debussy to say that the *Ring* struck him as a sort of vast musical city directory.

There are two kinds of *Leitmotiv* in Wagner: some symbolize abstract ideas (the Fate theme, the Vengeance theme, and so on); the others make the pretense of representing objects or concrete personages: the sword, for example, or the curious Nibelung family.

It is strange that skeptics who readily demand new proofs for everything and who usually take a sly delight in exposing whatever is purely conventional in established forms, never ask that any proof be given of the necessity or even of the simple expediency of any musical phrase that claims to identify itself with an idea, an object, or a character. If I am told that the power of genius is here great enough to justify this identification, then I shall ask what is the use of those widely circulated little guides that are the material embodiment of the musical city directory Debussy had in mind, little guides that make the neophyte attending a presentation of *Die Götterdämmerung* resemble one of those tourists you see on top of the Empire State Building trying to orient himself by spreading out a map of New York. And never let it be said that these little memory-books are an insult to Wagner and betray his thought: their wide circulation alone sufficiently proves that they answer a real need.

Basically, what is most irritating about these artistic rebels, of whom Wagner offers us the most complete type, is the spirit of systematization which, under the guise of doing away with conventions, establishes a new set, quite as arbitrary and much more cumbersome than the old. So that it is less the arbitrariness — which, all things considered, is fairly harmless — that tries our patience, than the system which this arbitrariness sets up as a principle. An example of this comes to mind. We have said that the object of music is not and cannot be imitation. But should it happen, for some purely accidental reason, that music makes an exception to this rule, this exception may in its turn become the origin of a convention. It thus offers the musician the possibility of using it as a commonplace. Verdi, in the famous thunderstorm in *Rigoletto*, did not hesitate to make use of a formula which many a composer had employed before him. Verdi applies his

78

own inventiveness to it and, without going outside of the tradition, makes out of a commonplace a perfectly original page that bears his unmistakable mark. You must agree that we are here very far from the Wagnerian system, exalted by its censer-bearers to the detriment of the Italianism which is treated with contempt by so many subtle thinkers who have gone astray in the symphonicism which is to them an endless pretext for literary glosses.

So the danger lies not in the borrowing of clichés. The danger lies in fabricating them and in bestowing on them the force of law, a tyranny that is merely a manifestation of romanticism grown decrepit.

Romanticism and classicism are terms that have been laden with such diverse meanings that you must not expect me to take sides in an endless argument which is most certainly becoming more and more an argument over words. This does not alter the fact that in a very general sense the principles of submission and insubordination which we have defined characterize by and large the attitude of the classicist and the romanticist before a work of art; a purely theoretic division, moreover, for we shall always find at the origin of invention an irrational element on which the spirit of submission has no hold and that escapes all constraint. That is what André Gide has so well expressed in saying that classical works are beautiful only by virtue of their subjugated romanticism. What is salient in this aphorism is the necessity for subjugation. Look at the work of Tschaikovsky for example.

Of what is it made up? And where did he find his sources if not in the arsenal that was currently made use of by the romantics? His themes are for the most part romantic — so is his driving impulse. What is not at all romantic is his attitude before the problem of incorporating them into the musical work. What could be more satisfying to our taste than the cut of his phrases and their beautiful arrangement? Please do not think that I am seeking a pretext to eulogize one of the few Russian composers of whom I am really fond. I take him as an example only because the example is so striking, just as the music of another romantic is striking, a romantic much further removed from us. I am speaking of Karl Maria von Weber. I am thinking of his sonatas which are of an instrumental bearing so formal that the few *rubati* which they permit themselves on occasion do not manage to conceal the constant and alert control of the subjugator. What a difference between *Der Freischütz*, *Euryanthe*, and *Oberon* on one hand and *Der Fliegende Holländer*, *Tannhäuser*, and *Lohengrin* with their laxness on the other. The contrast is striking. It is not just by chance, alas! that the latter works are much more often on the billboards of our theaters than the marvelous operas of Weber.

Summing up: What is important for the lucid ordering of the work — for its crystallization — is that all the Dionysian elements which set the imagination of the artist in motion and make the life-sap rise must be properly subjugated before they intoxicate us, and must finally be made to submit to the law: Apollo demands it.

It is far from my tastes, as well as from my intentions, to prolong further the endless debate over classicism and romanticism. I have said at sufficient length what I had to say to make my attitude clear on this subject; but I should leave my task unfinished if I did not call your attention for an instant to a closely related question, the question of those other two antagonists: modernism and academicism.

First of all, what an abortive neologism the word modernism is! Just what does it mean? In its most clearly defined meaning it designates a form of theological liberalism which is a fallacy condemned by the Church of Rome. Applied to the arts, would modernism be open to an analogous condemnation? I strongly think so . . . What is modern is what is representative of its own time and what must be in keeping with and within the grasp of its own time. Sometimes artists are reproached for being too modern or not modern enough. One might just as well reproach the times with not being sufficiently modern or with being too modern. A recent popular poll showed that, to all appearances, Beethoven is the composer most in demand in the United States. On that basis one can say that Beethoven is very modern and that a composer of such manifest importance as Paul Hindemith is not modern at all, since the list of winners does not even mention his name.

In itself, the term modernism implies neither praise

81

nor blame and involves no obligation whatsoever. That is precisely its weakness. The word eludes us, hiding under any application of it one wishes to make. True, it is said that one must live in one's own time. The advice is superfluous: how could one do otherwise? Even if I wanted to relive the past, the most energetic strivings of my misguided will would be futile.

It follows that everyone has taken advantage of the pliability of this vacuous term by trying to give it form and color. But, again, what do we understand by the term modernism? In the past the term was never used, was even unknown. Yet our predecessors were no more stupid than we are. Was the term a real discovery? We have shown that it was nothing of the sort. Might it not rather be a sign of a decadence in morality and taste? Here I strongly believe we must answer in the affirmative.

My fondest hope, to finish up, is that you may be as embarrassed by the expression as I myself am. It would be so much simpler to give up lying and admit once and for all that we call anything modern that caters to our snobbishness, in the true sense of the word. But is catering to snobbishness really worth the trouble?

The term modernism is all the more offensive in that it is usually coupled with another whose meaning is perfectly clear: I speak of academicism.

A work is called academic when it is composed strictly according to the precepts of the conservatory.

It follows that academicism considered as a scholastic exercise based on imitation is in itself something very useful and even indispensable to beginners who train themselves by studying models. It likewise follows that academicism should find no place outside of the conservatory and that those who make an ideal of academicism when they have already completed their studies produce stiffly correct works that are bloodless and dry.

Contemporary writers on music have acquired the habit of measuring everything in terms of modernism, that is to say in terms of a nonexistent scale, and promptly consign to the category of "academic" — which they regard as the opposite of modern — all that is not in keeping with the extravagances which in their eyes constitute the thrice-distilled quintessence of modernism. To these critics, whatever appears discordant and confused is automatically relegated to the pigeonhole of modernism. Whatever they cannot help finding clear and well-ordered, and devoid of ambiguity which might give them an opening, is promptly relegated in its turn to the pigeonhole of academicism. Now we can make use of academic forms without running the risk of becoming academic ourselves. The person who is loath to borrow these forms when he has need of them clearly betrays his weakness. How many times have I noticed this strange incomprehension on the part of those who believe themselves good judges of music and its future! What makes this all the more difficult to understand is the fact that these same critics admit as natural and legitimate the borrowing of old popular or religious melodies harmonized in ways incompatible with their essence. They are not at all shocked by the ridiculous device of the *Leitmotiv* and let themselves be inveigled into musical tours conducted by the Cook Agency of Bayreuth. They believe themselves up to the minute when they applaud the very introductory measures of a symphony employing exotic scales, obsolete instruments, and methods which were created for entirely different purposes. Terrified at the thought of showing themselves for what they are, they go after poor academicism tooth and nail, for they feel the same horror of forms consecrated by long use that their favorite composers feel, who are afraid to touch them.

Since I myself have so often borrowed academic attitudes with no thought of concealing the pleasure I found in them, I have not been spared becoming the chosen victim of these gentlemen's corrective rod.

My greatest enemies have always paid me the honor of recognizing that I am fully aware of what I am doing. The academic temperament cannot be acquired. One does not acquire a temperament. Now, I do not have a temperament suited to academicism; so I always use academic formulas knowingly and voluntarily. I use them quite as knowingly as I would use folklore. They are raw materials of my work. And I find it quite comical that my critics take an attitude that they cannot possibly maintain. For some day, willy-nilly, they will have to grant me what, out of pre-conceived notions, they have denied me.

I am no more academic than I am modern, no more modern than I am conservative. *Pulcinella* would suffice to prove this. So you ask just what I am? I refuse to expatiate upon the subject of my own person, which remains outside the objective of my course. And if I have allowed myself to talk to you a little about my own work, that was merely to illustrate my thought with an example at once personal and concrete. I can take other examples that will make up for my silence and my refusal to put myself on display. They will show you still more clearly how criticism through the ages has fulfilled its role as informant.

In 1737 the German writer on music, Scheibe, wrote of Bach: "This great man would be the object of world-wide admiration if he were more ingratiating and did not spoil his compositions with too much bombast and confusion; and if, by a surfeit of art he did not obscure their beauty."

Would you like to know what Schiller — the illustrious Schiller — wrote of Haydn's *Creation* in an account of a *soirée* where he heard it? "It is a hodge-podge without character. Haydn is a clever artist but lacks inspiration (*sic*). The whole thing is frigid."

Ludwig Spohr, a renowned composer, hears the Ninth Symphony thirty years after Beethoven's death and discovers in it a new argument in favor of what he had always said, namely, that Beethoven lacked an education in aesthetics and also "a sense of beauty."

That really isn't bad, but here is something even better. For the choice morsel we have saved up the poet Grillparzer's opinion of Weber's *Euryanthe*: "A complete lack of order and color. This music is hideous. Such a perversion of euphony, such a rape of the beautiful would have been punished by law in the great age of Greece. Such music should come under police jurisdiction . . ."

Such quotations keep me from committing the folly of defending myself against the incompetence of my critics and of complaining about the slight interest they take in my efforts.

I do not mean to question the critics' rights. On the contrary, I regret that they exercise them so little and often so inappropriately.

"Criticism," says the dictionary, "is the art of judging literary productions and works of art." We gladly adopt this definition. Therefore, since criticism is an art, it cannot itself escape our criticisms. What do we ask of it? What limits shall we assign to its domain? In truth, we want it to be entirely free in its proper functioning which consists of judging existing works and not of maundering over the legitimacy of their origins or intentions.

A composer has the right to expect that criticism shall at least acknowledge the opportunity which he provides for judging his work at its face value. What is the point in endlessly questioning the very principle of operation? What is the use of wearing out the composer with superfluous questions, by asking him why he has chosen a certain subject, a certain argument, a certain voice, a certain instrumental form? What is the use, in a word, of tormenting him with the *why* instead of seeking for itself the *how*, and thus establishing the reasons for his failure or success?

It is obviously much easier to ask questions than to give answers. It is easier to question than to explain.

It is my conviction that the public always shows itself more honest in its spontaneity than do those who officially set themselves up as judges of works of art. You may believe a man who in the course of his career has had occasion to become acquainted with the most varied publics; and I have been able to note for myself in my double role as composer and performer that the less the public was predisposed favorably or unfavorably towards a musical work, the more healthy were its reactions to the work and the more propitious to the development of the art of music.

After the failure of his most recent play, a man of wit declared that the public had decidedly less and less talent . . . I think, on the contrary, that it is the composers who sometimes lack talent and that the public always has, if not talent (which could hardly be the adjunct of a collective body), at least, when it is left to itself, a spontaneity that confers great value upon its reactions. Provided again that it has not been contaminated with the virus of snobbery.

I have often heard artists say: "Why do you complain about snobs? It is they who are the most useful servants of new trends. If they don't serve them out of conviction, they do it at least in their capacity as snobs. They are your best customers." I answer that they are bad customers, false customers, since they are as readily at the service of error as of truth. By serving all causes they completely vitiate the best ones, because they confuse them with the worst.

All things considered, I prefer the forthright invective of the simple listener who has understood nothing to all the hollow praises that are as completely meaningless to those who proffer them as to those who receive them.

Like every sort of evil, snobbery tends to give rise to another evil which is its opposite: *pompierisme.** When all is said and done, the snob is himself nothing but a sort of *pompier* — a vanguard *pompier*.

The vanguard *pompiers* make small talk about music just as they do about Freudianism or Marxism. At the slightest provocation they bring up the *complexes* of psychoanalysis and even go so far today as to familiarize themselves, albeit reluctantly — but *snobisme oblige* — with the great Saint Thomas Aquinas . . . All things considered, to that sort of *pompier* I prefer the pure and simple *pompier* who talks about melody and, with hand over heart, champions the incontestable rights of sentiment, defends the primacy of emotion, gives evidence of concern for the noble, on occasion

* The word "pompier" originated with the resemblance in mid-nineteenth century pictures of the casques of ancient Roman officials to firemen's helmets. It is now applied to persons who represent pompous pedantry and officialdom.

yields to the adventure or oriental picturesqueness, and even goes so far as to praise my *Firebird*. You will readily understand that it is not for this reason that I prefer him to the other sort of *pompier* . . . It is simply that I find him less dangerous. The vanguard *pompiers*, moreover, make the mistake of being contemptuous beyond all measure of their colleagues of yesteryear. Both will remain *pompiers* all their lives, and the revolutionary ones go out of style more quickly than the others: time is a greater threat to them.

The true music-lover, like the true patron, does not fit into these categories; but like every authentic thing of worth, both are rare. The false patron is ordinarily recruited from the rank of the snobs, just as the old-fashioned *pompier* is usually recruited from the *bourgeoisie*.

For reasons I have already given, the bourgeois irritates me much less than the snob. And I am not defending the bourgeois when I say that it is really too easy to attack him. We shall leave those attacks to the great specialists in this matter — the communists. From the point of view of humanism and the development of the spirit, it goes without saying that the bourgeois constitutes an obstacle and a danger. But that danger is too well known to disquiet us in the same measure as the danger that is never denounced as such: snobbery.

It is impossible, in concluding, not to say a word or two about the patron that has played a role of prime importance in the development of the arts. The harshness of the times and the all-engulfing demagoguery that tend to transform the state into an anonymous and senselessly leveling patron make us long for the Margrave of Brandenburg who was helpful to Johann Sebastian Bach, for Prince Esterhazy who looked after Haydn, and for Louis II of Bavaria who protected Wagner. Though art patronage grows weaker day by day, let us honor the few patrons that remain to us, from the poor patron who feels he has done enough for the artist when he has offered him a cup of tea in exchange for his gracious contribution, to the anonymous Dives who, having delegated the job of distributing largess to the secretariat in charge of the department of munificence, thus becomes a patron without knowing it.

5. THE AVATARS OF RUSSIAN MUSIC

WHY DO WE ALWAYS
hear Russian music spoken of in terms of its Russian-
ness rather than simply in terms of music? Because
it is always the picturesque, the strange rhythms, the
timbres of the orchestra, the orientalism — in short, the
local color, that is seized upon; because people are
interested in everything that goes to make up the Russian, or supposedly Russian, setting: *troïka, vodka,
isba, balalaika, pope, boyar, samovar, nitchevo,* and
even bolshevism. For bolshevism offers similar dis-
plays which, however, bear names that conform more
closely to the exigencies of its doctrines.

I hope you will be so good as to permit me to consider Russia from another point of view . . . My express purpose is to help clear up a misapprehension
of long-standing to correct certain distortions of perspective. If I have seen fit to devote one session of my
course to Russian music, it is not because I am particularly fond of it by reason of my origins; it is chiefly
because the music of Russia, particularly in its latest
developments, illustrates in a characteristic and very
significant way the principal theses that I desire to

present to you. I shall thus devote less time to an historical view of Russian music than to what I have called its avatars — its transformations during the course of the very brief period that comprises its whole existence. For its beginnings as an art conscious of itself do not go back for more than a hundred years or so, and it is customarily agreed that these beginnings are inseparable from the first works of Glinka.

From Glinka on we can observe the use of folklore in Russian music. It is in the opera *A Life for the Czar* that the *melos* of the people is quite naturally incorporated into art music. Glinka is not here obeying the dictates of custom. He does not think of laying the groundwork of a vast enterprise for export purposes: he takes the popular *motif* as raw material and treats it quite instinctively according to the usages of the Italian music then in vogue. Glinka does not hobnob with the common people, as certain of his successors did, to reinforce his vigor through contact with the plain truth. He is merely looking for elements of musical enjoyment. Out of a culture acquired through contact with the Italians, he always retained a natural taste for Italian music, and it is without any desire to establish a system that he introduced into his works melodies of popular origin or feeling.

Dargomyzhski, a talent less forceful, less original, but of the finest sort, shows similar tastes. His charming opera *Roussalka*, his delightful *romanzas* and songs likewise mingle the Russian popular *melos* and the prevailing Italianism with the most carefree and charming ease.

The Five, Slavophiles of the populist variety, were to set up this unconscious utilization of folklore as a system. Their ideas and their tastes inclined them toward a kind of devotion for the people's cause, a tendency which, of course, had not yet taken on the vast proportions that it has in our day in conformity with the instructions of the Third International.

Balakirev, Moussorgsky, Borodin, Rimski-Korsakov, to whom we must add the less characteristic personality of César Cui, all seize upon popular melodies and liturgical chants.

So, with the best of intentions — and with varying degrees of talent — The Five sought to graft the popular strain upon art music. At the outset, the freshness of their ideas made up for the inadequacy of their technique. But freshness is not easily reproduced. The moment arrived when the need was felt to consolidate achievements, and to that end, to perfect technique. From the amateurs that all of them were at the outset of their movement, they changed to professionals and lost the first fine careless rapture of youth that was their charm.

That was how Rimski-Korsakov came to embark on a methodic study of compositon and broke with the amateurism of his colleagues to become himself an eminent teacher.

In that capacity he set up an active center of genuinely professional composers, thereby laying the foundations for the most solid and most estimable academic instruction. I was able to enjoy for myself the benefits of his sober and forceful pedagogic gift.

Around the eighties, a rich amateur, Belyaev, who turned publisher out of love for Russian music, brought together a small circle of musicians which included Rimski-Korsakov, his young and brilliant pupil Glazunov, Liadov, and a few other composers. Under cover of concern for the most serious of professional techniques, their works gave evidence of the alarming symptoms of a new academicism. The Belyaev circle, then, turned more and more towards academicism. Italianism, renounced and reviled, gave way to an ever-increasing enthusiasm for German technique, and it is not without reason that Glazunov has been called the Russian Brahms.

The nucleus made up by the group of The Five found opposition in another quarter where, simply by virtue of the brilliance of his powerful talent, the personality of Tchaikovsky shone forth all alone. Tchaikovsky, like Rimski-Korsakov, was aware of the necessity of acquiring a solid technique; both were conservatory teachers, Rimski at Saint Petersburg, Tchaikovsky at Moscow. But the latter's musical language is as completely apart from the prejudices that characterized The Five as Glinka's had been. Whereas Glinka lived during the reign of the opera and Italian song, Tchaikovsky, who appears at the end of this reign and whose formation had been determined by it, did not have an exclusive admiration for Italian music.

His formal education had been conducted along the lines of the German academies. But if he was not ashamed of liking Schumann and Mendelssohn, whose music obviously influenced his symphonic work, his sympathies went out with a sort of predilection to Gounod, Bizet, and Delibes, his French contemporaries. Nevertheless, however attentive and sensitive he was to the world outside of Russia, one can say that he generally showed himself to be, if not nationalist and populist like The Five, at least profoundly national in the character of his themes, the cut of his phrases, and the rhythmic physiognomy of his work.

I have spoken to you of the Russian Glinka who embraced Italy, of the Russian Five who wed national folklore to the naturalistic realism dear to their epoch, and of the Russian Tchaikovsky, who found his true expression by turning with open arms to occidental culture.

Whatever one may think of these tendencies, they were comprehensible and legitimate. They obeyed a certain order. They took their place within the framework of Russian history. Unfortunately, academicism, the first signs of which were visible in the activity of the Belyaev circle, was not long in gathering *epigoni*, while the imitators of Tchaikovsky degenerated into a mawkish lyricism. But just when one might have thought we were on the eve of a dictatorship of conservatism, a new disorder had wormed its way into Russian thought, a disorder whose beginnings were marked by the success of theosophy; an ideological, psychological, and sociological disorder that took possession of music with impudent unconcern. For, frankly, is it possible to connect a musician like Scriabin with any tradition whatsoever? Where does he come from? And who are his forebears?

So we are brought to consider two Russias, a Russia of the right and a Russia of the left, which embody two kinds of disorder: conservative disorder and revolutionary disorder. What has been the upshot of these two disorders? The history of the last twenty years will assume the burden of showing us.

We shall see revolutionary disorder devour conservative disorder, and, devouring, develop such a taste for the dish that it will ask for more, and always keep asking for more — until it dies of indigestion.

And this brings me to the second part of my lesson: Soviet Russian music will be its subject-matter.

First of all, I must confess that I know it only from a distance. But did not Gogol say that from a distant land (in this case, Italy, his adopted country) "it was easier for him to embrace Russia in all its vastness"? I too believe I have some right to judge it from a west European or American vantage point. All the more so because Russia, at the present moment, is wrestling with processes so contradictory that it is admittedly almost impossible to see clearly from a close vantage point, and consequently all the more impossible from the interior of the country itself.

Music is what I am going to speak about, but before I do that, it is absolutely essential in order that this

98

particular problem may be the better delimited and placed, that I say a few words to you in very general terms about the Russian Revolution.

What strikes us above all is that the Revolution came at a time when Russia seemed to have freed itself once and for all (at least in principle) both from the psychosis of materialism and from the revolutionary ideas that had enslaved it since the middle of the nineteenth century up until the first revolution of 1905. In truth, the nihilism, the revolutionary cult of the common people, the rudimentary materialism, as well as the shady plots hatched in the underworld of terrorism, had little by little disappeared. By that time Russia had already become enriched with new philosophic ideas. She had undertaken researches into her own historical and religious life, researches attributable chiefly to Leontiev, Soloviëv, Rosanov, Berdyaev, Fedorov, and Nesmelov. On the other hand, the literary "Symbolism" that we connect with the names of Blok, Z. Guippius, and Bely, as well as the artistic movement "Mir Iskoustva" of Diaghilev, had contributed much to this enrichment. Not to mention what was then called "legalistic Marxism," which had supplanted the revolutionary Marxism of Lenin and the exiles grouped around him.

Certainly, this "Russian Renaissance" might appear inorganic and impotent in many aspects; we have all the more reason to judge it thus today.

One has only to recall the grotesque movement led by Tchoulkov which was called "The Movement of

Mystical Anarchists" — a thoroughly suspect mysticism, moreover — and recall Merezhkovski and the significant success of Andreyev and Artzybasheff, novelists in the worst possible taste. Yet, compared to the dark period of the years 1860 to 1880, the period of the Chernyshevskies, the Dobrolyubovs, the Pissarevs, when a perfidious wave that defiled the true foundations of culture and the state welled up from the milieu of false intellectuals, morally disinherited and socially uprooted, and from the centers of atheistic seminarists and flunked-out students — compared to that period, the twenty years that preceded the Revolution justifiably seem to us a short period of convalescence and renewal.

Alas, that cultural renaissance did not find a commensurate expression in the sphere of governmental reforms nor in the domain of economic initiative and social problems — so that at the outset of the World War, Russian society was still made of paradoxically disparate elements such as the feudal order (still extant at that moment), occidental capitalism, and a primitive communism (in the form of rural communities). It is not surprising, therefore, that at the first shock (in this case, the World War) this system, if one can call it a system, could not withstand external and internal pressure. Thus, the nascent Revolution, which united the Marxist radicalism of the exiles with the agrarian "pogrom" and the confiscation of private property, was to overturn and trample upon all the superstructures of the pre-war culture, by that very act reducing Russia to the lowly rank of Dostoievski's "Demons" and plunging it once again into a militant atheism and a rudimentary materialism.

One might say that there took place at that time a tragic collision of *two disorders*. To revolutionary disorder the weak and lax government could only oppose another disorder, a reactionary one. Neither the authorities nor social conscience was equal to the task of realizing or even of formulating a live and constructive system of counteraction capable of curbing and disarming the pressure of the revolutionary forces which, nevertheless, had appreciably weakened around 1910, having lost a good deal of ground through their subversive propaganda. In truth, it seems impossible to explain such an atrophying of the Russian state when, drawing on an age-old tradition, it was fundamentally tending to realize the idea of a Third Rome. As Rosanov's felicitous image puts it, "Russia lost its colors in three days, if not in two."

It seems high time to give up the banal and erroneous point of view (one, moreover, that has so often been given the lie by the facts) which attributes to the Russian type an element of innate irrationality, claiming to find therein the explanation of the Russian's predispositions towards mysticism and religious devotion. Even granting the Russian that peculiarity, one could not without temerity stop there and neglect another side of this same nature, namely the tendencies to a rudimentary and almost childlike rationalism that frequently degenerates into fault-finding and sterile

101

disputation. This too is a specifically Russian characteristic.

In the spiritual realm, this other side has brought about militant atheism as well as the rationalistic doctrines of the religious sects, sects which, moreover, still exist in our day side by side with the official atheism of the communists. This rationalism, and its pseudo-critical spirit have poisoned and continue to poison the whole field of art in Russia, with the famous arguments over the "meaning of Art" and of "what is Art and what is its Mission?"

It was right after Pushkin's death and primarily through Gogol that such speculations seeped into the Russian mind. Russian art has suffered considerable damage from them. Some saw the intrinsic reason for Art as the abandonment and disdain of the customs and usages of life. In this connection I call your attention to the famous movement of the "Peredvijniki," with its traveling exhibitions, a movement that preceded Diaghilev's effort.

Others denied art any right to be an end in itself. Witness to this is the famous discussion that was taken so seriously around the 1860's: "Which is the more important, Shakespeare or a pair of boots?" Even Tolstoy in his aesthetic vagaries wandered off into the impasse of morals and its categorical imperative. This is to be connected with his total incomprehension of the genesis of any kind of creation. Finally, the Marxist theory that maintains that art is only a "superstructure based on conditions of production" has had as a consequence that art in Russia is nothing more than an instrument of political propaganda at the service of the Communist Party and the government. Of course, such a corruption of the Russian critical spirit has not spared music. Down to the first ten years of the twentieth century, Glinka's successors, with the exception of Tschaikovsky, all in varying degrees paid tribute either to the ideas of populism or to revolutionary ideas or, finally, to folklore, and all of them assigned to music problems and aims that are foreign to it. I shall cite, by way of a curiosity, this little known fact: namely, that Scriabin had intended to put an epigraph on the erotico-mystical score of his "Poem of Ecstasy," an epigraph that was none other than the "Arise, ye wretched of the earth," the first sentence of the original French version of the "Internationale."

Only a few years before the war did music in Russia undertake to emancipate itself to some degree. It tended to break away from the tutelage of The Five and especially from the Rimski-Korsakov school which at that moment, as we have said, represented nothing more than a rigid academicism. The war was to shatter these efforts, and subsequent events swept away its last vestiges. Thus the Revolution found Russian music completely disoriented, within its own country, that is, so that the Bolsheviks had no trouble at all in directing its development to their own liking and profit.

To tell the truth, Russian art before the October Revolution had held aloof from revolutionary Marxism. The late-comers of symbolism as well as all the younger

103

imitators grouped around them accepted the revolution without by any means becoming its torch-bearers. Gorki, a personal friend of some of the communist leaders, went into exile at Sorrento a few years after the establishment of communism, where he remained for quite a long while, to return to Russia only shortly before his death, which occurred in 1936. This long absence even provoked an acid diatribe from the futurist poet Mayakovski which he addressed to Gorki around 1926 in the form of an epistle in verse — "What a pity, Comrade Gorki," he said, "that we never meet you these days in the workshops. Maybe you feel you can see things more clearly from the hills of Capri?"

Strange as it may seem, in the beginning futurism alone, even though it incurred a rebuke from Lenin himself, embraced the views of communism. Mayakovski in poetry and Meyerhold in the theater were its principal protagonists. As for music, it did not find comparable leaders. Then too, during the first years of the Revolution, musical policy restricted itself to rudimentary decrees by sanctioning one or another work by bourgeois composers (that was the consecrated term). This is about how things went: Rimski-Korsakov's *Kitesh*, considered too mystical, was put on the index, whereas Tchaikovsky's *Eugene Onegin*, recognized as an opera that portrayed manners realistically, was given the honor of being performed. Shortly afterwards it was just the opposite. *Kitesh* was discovered to be a popular drama, thus worthy of being sanctioned. As for *Eugene Onegin*, it gave off a perfume of feudal nobility, so it was stricken from the repertory . . .

I shall cite still another curious fact of that period: the founding of the conductorless orchestra, Persimfans (first symphonic ensemble), which somewhat naïvely symbolized the collective principle in opposition to the so-called authoritarian and dictatorial principle which requires the aid of a conductor. Since then, as you will easily understand, many things have changed in Russian life.

During the first period of Bolshevism, the public authorities were much too busy with other things to concern themselves with art in a systematic fashion. And art itself was prey to the most diverse and contradictory theories. These theories, in truth, were derived from the domain of extravagant fantasy, or even of the ridiculous. That is how it came about that opera in general was denounced as useless. The originators of that assertion took their argument from the supposedly religious and feudal origin of the operatic genre (*sic*) and from its conventional character. Opera as a form, in addition, seemed to defy artistic realism, the slowness of its action corresponding in no way to the tempo of the new socialist way of life. Some maintained that only the masses could be the principal character, the hero of the opera, or that the revolutionary opera should not be concerned with any plot at all. These theories, furthermore, enjoyed a certain success; a fact proved by the composition of quite a series of operas according to the principles of mass-opera and plotless-opera. For example, Dechevoff's *Ice and Steel* and Gladkowsky's *The Front and the Rear.* Independently of these regional and provincial ideologies, so typically Russian, a revolutionary and romantic cult was dedicated to Beethoven. In performance the Finale of the Ninth Symphony was often played in conjunction with the "Internationale," composed, as you know, by the Belgian Degeyter. Lenin, for some unknown reason, found in the Appassionata sonata "superhuman music." Beethoven was considered in the light of the ideas of Romain Rolland, who, as you know, heard "saber-clashings," the noise of battle, and the lamentations of the vanquished in the Eroica.

Here, written by one of the most celebrated Soviet music critics, is an analysis of this same Third Symphony.

The violins, in hushed voices, intone their somber and grief-stricken song. The voice of the oboe, steeped in sadness, rises steadily. Then the warriors, in austere silence [?] accompany their leader to his last resting-place. But here there is no despair. Beethoven the optimist, the great lover of Life, had too high a regard for man to repeat the contemptuous [?!] words of the Christian Church: "Dust thou art and unto dust shalt thou return!"

In the Scherzo and the Finale Beethoven shouts in a voice of thunder: "No, thou art not dust, but indeed the Master of the Earth." And once again the dazzling image of the hero comes to life in the spirited scherzo, as well as in the tempestuous and shattering finale.

Any commentary on commentaries of this sort seems superfluous.

In one of his articles another critic and musicologist,

even more prominent and famous than the one just quoted, reassures us that "Beethoven battled to defend the civil rights of music as art, and his works betray no tendency to aristocratism."

As you can see, all this has nothing to do either with Beethoven, or with music, or with true musical criticism.

Today, then, just as in the past, in the times of Stasov and Moussorgsky (a musician of genius, assuredly, but always confused in his ideas) the reasoning "intelligentsia" seeks to assign a role to music and to attribute to it a meaning totally foreign to its true mission. A meaning from which music is in truth very far removed.

So much exaggerated ambitiousness and grandiloquence do not alter the fact that *Eugene Onegin* is still the opera the public loves best, the one which replenishes the till (even though there are state subsidies). It was necessary, nevertheless, in order to rehabilitate the opera, for Lunacharski (Commissar of Fine Arts and Public Instruction) to point out (and this is quite comic) that the conflict of two lovers does in no way contradict the ideas of communism.

I am trying to give you a succinct view of the present-day situation of Soviet music and of the theories and tendencies that have taken shape around it — but I must pause once more to consider two facts.

Twice Stalin has personally and openly taken a hand in the matter of Soviet art. The first time was in connection with Mayakovski. Everyone knows that the poet's suicide in 1930 had profoundly disturbed and bewildered the most orthodox communists, provoking a veritable insurrection in his name, for the persecution of Mayakovski had begun several years before his death and was grounded on the disapproval of all "leftish" tendencies of literature in general. In order to restore full prestige and significance to Mayakovski's name, nothing less than Stalin's personal intervention would do. "Mayakovski," he said, "is the greatest and best (*sic*) poet of the Soviet epoch." And the epithet, of course, became classic and passed from mouth to mouth. If I have paused for a moment over this literary incident, I do it first of all because the chair of Poetics which I occupy at this moment authorizes me, I believe, to do so, and secondly because, compared to the tumultuous life of Soviet literature, music has remained in the shade, in the background.

However, the second intervention by Stalin is connected precisely with music. It was brought about by the scandals provoked by Shostakovich's opera *Lady Macbeth of Mtsensk* on a subject taken from Leskov, and by his ballet "The Limpid Brook" on the themes of the Kolkhos (Collective Farm). Shostakovich's music and the subject-matter of his compositions were severely censured, perhaps not altogether wrongly this time. They were additionally attacked as being decrepit formalism. The performance of his music was forbidden, thus joining the ranks of the music of Hindemith, Schoenberg, Alban Berg, and other European composers.

108

I must tell you that there were reasons for this war against so-called difficult music.

After the periods of romanticism, constructivism, and futurism had run their course, and after interminable discussions on themes such as "Jazz or Symphony?", and also as a consequence of the mania for everything grandiose, artistic consciousness broke abruptly with the leftist formulas, for clearly political and social reasons, and followed the paths of "simplification," and the new popularism and folklore.

The vogue for the composer Dzerjinsky, abetted by Stalin's personal approval, as well as by the success of his operas on subjects taken from Sholokhov's novels *The Silent Don* and *Seeds of Tomorrow* revealed this self-styled "new" trend towards popular folklore, a trend in reality long familiar to Russian music, and in which it persists to this very day.

I am purposely not spending any time on the works and activity of the composers who had already been formed and become known before the Revolution and who have since undergone no marked development (for example, Miaskovski, Steinberg, and others who are merely the followers of the Rimski-Korsakov and Glazunov schools).

It is maintained in Russia today that the new listener of the masses requires a simple and comprehensible music. The order of the day for all the arts is "socialist realism." On the other hand, the national policy of the Soviet Union encourages in a thousand ways the regional artistic production of the eleven republics included in the system of the Union. These two facts alone have determined the style, form, and tendencies of contemporary Soviet music.

Within a few years a quantity of collections has appeared made up of the most varied folk songs (Ukrainian, Georgian, Armenian, Azerbaijanian, Abkhasian, Buriato-Mongol, Tartar, Kalmuk, Turkmenian, Kirghiz, Hebraic, and so on). As interesting and important as this ethnographical and taxonomic work may be in itself, it should not be confused, as is the case in Soviet Russia, with problems of culture and musical creation, for these have very little to do with ethnographic expeditions. All the more so in view of the fact that these expeditions have as their prescribed aim to notate and bring back thousands of songs on Stalin, Voroshilov, and the other leaders. All the more reason why musical creativeness does not enter into the unfailingly conventional and often suspect harmonizations of these folk songs.

At the same time, it is noteworthy that the clearly political interests that are constantly brought to bear on musical folklore should go hand in hand, as is always the case in Russia, with a confused and complicated theory expressly pointing out that "the different regional cultures are evolving and broadening into a musical culture of the whole great socialist country."

Here is what one of the most outstanding of Soviet music critics and musicologists writes: "It is high time that we abandon the distinction — entirely feudal, bourgeois, and pretentious — between folk music and

110

artistic music. As if the quality of being aesthetic were only the privilege of the individual invention and personal creation of the composer." If the growing interest in musical ethnography is bought at the price of such heresies, it would perhaps be preferable that this interest be exercised on the pre-revolutionary primitive musical forms, otherwise it runs the risk of bringing only harm and confusion to Russian music.

This fad for folklore gave rise nonetheless to a whole series of compositions, small and large, such as the operas *Schah-Sénem, Gulsara, Daïssi, Abessalom and Eteri, Aïtchourek, Adjal-Ordouna, Altine-Kiz, Tarass-Boulba*, and so on. All these compositions belong to the conventional type of opera. Of course they solve no creative problem, for they belong to the category of "official" art and affect a pseudo-popular idiom. One can add in this connection the recent fad for the "Ukranian" operetta that formerly was called the "Little Russian" operetta.

If the overseers of Soviet music confuse, wilfully or perhaps through ignorance, the problems of ethnography with those of creativeness, they commit the same error in the matter of performance, since they elevate it for tendentious reasons to the level of a creative phenomenon and of true musical culture. The same holds true for those amateur groups of all sorts that form orchestras, choruses, and popular ensembles which are always cited as an argument to prove the development of the artistic powers of the peoples of the Union. Certainly it is fine that Soviet pianists and violinists carry off first prizes in international competitions (insofar as such competitions have ever had any value whatsoever or contributed anything at all to music). Certainly it is fine that Russia should perform her folk dances and cultivate songs of the Kolkhosi. But is it possible to linger over these secondary matters in the hope of finding in such quantitative factors the signs of a true and genuine culture whose sources and conditions, just as in all the other fields of creation, are not at all contained in this mass consumption, which looks more like a result of drilling? Are such signs not to be found in something entirely different, something which Soviet Russia has completely forgotten or whose language she has unlearned?

I must finally direct your attention to two trends which, in my opinion, throw light on the musical tendencies of contemporary Russia all the better in that they are becoming more and more pronounced in recent years. These trends are, on the one hand, the reinforcing of the Thematics of the Revolution, the need for revolutionary subjects of immediate interest to the present day; and on the other hand, the rather specialized adaptation of classical works — still unprecedented elsewhere — to the requirements of contemporary life. After utilizing Sholokhov's novels as a source of operatic subjects, they have turned to Gorki and to civil-war subjects. In a new opera, *In the Storm*, they have even reached the point of making Lenin appear on the stage. As for the famous adaptations which I have just mentioned, I can tell you that quite recently the "Nutcracker" of Tchaikovsky was restored to the ballet repertory, not without modifying its plot and libretto, which were found to be of too mystical a coloring and thus dangerous, as well as foreign, to the Soviet spectator. In a like manner, after endless hesitations and numerous revisions, Glinka's celebrated opera *A Life for the Czar* has once more taken place in the repertory under the title of *Ivan Soussanine.* The word "Czar" was replaced as the occasion required by the words "Country," "Homeland," and "People." As for the Apotheosis, the original stage setting was retained with the traditional chimes and the processions of the clergy in their golden chasubles. One should not seek an explanation for this patriotic setting in Glinka's music, but rather in the national-defense propaganda. Lacking any authentic forms of expression of its own, the communist patriotism imposed upon the Soviet government by the pressure of events ("Thou thinkest to press, and thou art pressed") expressed itself, via subversion, through one of the purest masterpieces of classical Russian music, a masterpiece which had been conceived and composed in entirely different circumstances and embodied an entirely different meaning.

If the musical culture of contemporary Russia were as flourishing as is maintained, what need was there to have recourse to this borrowing from, I might even say this falsification of, Glinka?

The present problem of communist Russia, as you certainly understand, is above all a problem of general concepts, that is to say, of a system of comprehending and estimating values. It is the problem of choosing and singling-out the admissible from the inadmissible; a synthesis of experience with its consequences, in other words with its conclusions, which determine the taste and style of all life, of all action. From which I conclude that a general concept is, in truth, not capable of evolving, being in itself a closed circle. One can only remain inside it or step outside it. That is exactly the case with the communistic concept. For those who are held inside the circle, every question, every answer is determined in advance.

To sum up, I should like to say this. According to the present Russian mentality, there are basically two formulas that explain what music is. One kind of music would be in a more or less profane style, the other in an elevated or grandiloquent style. Kolkhosians surrounded by tractors and automachines (that is the term) dancing with a reasonable gaiety (in keeping with the requirements of communist dignity) to the accompaniment of a people's chorus: that will give an adequate picture of the first kind. To do this for the other kind, in elevated style, is far more complicated. Here music is called upon "to contribute to the formation of the human personality imbued with the environment of its great epoch."

One of the writers most esteemed by the Soviets, Alexis Tolstoy, does not hesitate to write with the greatest seriousness in reference to Shostakovich's Fifth Symphony.

114

Music must present the consummate formulation of the psychological tribulations of mankind, it should accumulate man's energy.

Here we have the "Symphony of Socialism." It begins with the *Largo* of the masses working underground, an *accellerando* corresponds to the subway system; the *Allegro* in its turn symbolizes gigantic factory machinery and its victory over nature. The *Adagio* represents the synthesis of Soviet culture, science, and art. The *Scherzo* reflects the athletic life of the happy inhabitants of the Union. As for the *Finale*, it is the image of the gratitude and the enthusiasm of the masses.

What I have just read to you is not a joke which I myself thought up. It is a literal quotation from a musicologist of repute which recently appeared in an official communist organ. It is in its line a consummate masterpiece of bad taste, mental infirmity, and complete disorientation in the recognition of the fundamental values of life. Nor is it any the less the result (if not the consequence) of a stupid concept. To see clearly, one would have to free one's self from it.

As for myself, you will readily understand, I consider these two formulas, these two images, to be equally inadmissible and hold them to be a nightmare. Music is not a "dancing Kolkhos" any more than it is a "Symphony of Socialism." What it really is I have tried to tell you in the course of my preceding lessons.

Perhaps these considerations seem to you full of harshness and bitterness. Indeed they are. But what surpasses all else is the amazement, I might even say stupefaction, into which the problem of Russia's his-

115

torical fate has always plunged me, a problem that has for centuries remained a mystery.

The great controversy of the "Slavophiles" and the "Occidentals" which has become the principal theme of all Russian philosophy and all Russian culture has, so to speak, solved nothing.

Both these opposing systems failed in a like measure in the cataclysm of the Revolution.

In spite of all the Messianic prophecies of the "Slavophiles" — who envisioned for Russia an historic road entirely new and independent of old Europe, before whom these "Slavophiles" bowed down only as before a sacred tomb — the communist Revolution has thrown Russia into the arms of Marxism, an occidental and European system par excellence. But what confounds us completely is that this hyperinternational system is itself quite rapidly undergoing transformation, and we see Russia falling back into an attitude of the worst sort of nationalism and popular chauvinism which once more separates it radically from European culture.

This means that after twenty-one years of catastrophic revolution, Russia could not and would not solve its great historical problem. Besides, how would she ever have accomplished this when she has never been capable of stabilizing her culture nor of consolidating her traditions? She finds herself, as she has always found herself, at a crossroads, facing Europe, yet turning her back upon it.

In the different cycles of its development and historical metamorphoses, Russia has ever been untrue to herself, she has always sapped the foundations of her own culture and profaned the values of the phases that have gone before.

And now that it comes about, through necessity, that she is once more taking up her traditions, she is content with their mere simulacrum without understanding that their intrinsic value, their very life have completely disappeared. That is the crux of this great tragedy.

A *renewal* is fruitful only when it goes hand in hand with *tradition*. Living dialectic wills that renewal and tradition shall develop and abet each other in a simultaneous process. Now Russia has seen only *conservatism* without *renewal* or *revolution* without *tradition*, whence arises the terrifying reeling over the void that has always made my head swim.

Do not be surprised to hear me terminate this lesson with such general considerations; but, whatever the case may be, art is not and cannot be "a superstructure based on conditions of production" in accordance with the wishes of the Marxists. Art is an ontological reality and, in attempting to understand the phenomenon of Russian music, I could not avoid making my analysis more general.

Without doubt the Russian people are among those most gifted for music. Unfortunately, though the Russian may know how to reason, cogitation and speculation are hardly his strong points. Now, without a speculative system, and lacking a well-defined order in cogitation, music has no value, or even existence, as art.

117

If the reeling of Russia through the course of history disorients me to the point of making my head swim, the perspectives of Russian musical art disconcert me no less. For art presupposes a culture, an upbringing, an integral stability of the intellect, and Russia of today has never been more completely devoid of these.

6. THE PERFORMANCE OF MUSIC

T IS NECESSARY TO DISTINGUISH two moments, or rather two states of music: potential music and actual music. Having been fixed on paper or retained in the memory, music exists already prior to its actual performance, differing in this respect from all the other arts, just as it differs from them, as we have seen, in the categories that determine its perception.

The musical entity thus presents the remarkable singularity of embodying two aspects, of existing successively and distinctly in two forms separated from each other by the hiatus of silence. This peculiar nature of music determines its very life as well as its repercussions in the social world, since it presupposes two kinds of musicians: the creator and the performer.

Let us note in passing that the art of the theater which requires the composition of a text and its translation into oral and visual terms, poses a similar, if not absolutely identical, problem; for there is a distinction that cannot be ignored: the theater appeals to our understanding by addressing itself simultaneously to sight and hearing. Now of all our senses sight is the most closely allied to the intellect, and hearing is appealed to in this case through articulated language, the vehicle for images and concepts. So the reader of a dramatic work can more easily imagine what its actual presentation would be like than the reader of a musical score can imagine how the actual instrumental playing of the score would sound. And it is easy to see why there are far fewer readers of orchestral scores than there are readers of books about music.

In addition, the language of music is strictly limited by its notation. The dramatic actor thus finds he has much more latitude in regard to *chronos* and intonation than does the singer who is tightly bound to *tempo* and *melos.*

This subjection, that is often so trying to the exhibitionism of certain soloists, is at the very heart of the question that we propose to take up now: the question of the executant and the interpreter.

The idea of interpretation implies the limitations imposed upon the performer or those which the performer imposes upon himself in his proper function, which is to transmit music to the listener.

The idea of execution implies the strict putting into effect of an explicit will that contains nothing beyond what it specifically commands.

It is the conflict of these two principles — execution and interpretation — that is at the root of all the errors, all the sins, all the misunderstandings that interpose themselves between the musical work and the listener and prevent a faithful transmission of its message.

Every interpreter is also of necessity an executant. The reverse is not true. Following the order of succession rather than of precedence, we shall first consider the executant.

It is taken for granted that I place before the performer written music wherein the composer's will is explicit and easily discernable from a correctly established text. But no matter how scrupulously a piece of music may be notated, no matter how carefully it may be insured against every possible ambiguity through the indications of *tempo*, shading, phrasing, accentuation, and so on, it always contains hidden elements that defy definition, because verbal dialectic is powerless to define musical dialectic in its totality. The realization of these elements is thus a matter of experience and intuition, in a word, of the talent of the person who is called upon to present the music.

Thus, in contrast to the craftsman of the plastic arts, whose finished work is presented to the public eye in an always identical form, the composer runs a perilous risk every time his music is played, since the competent presentation of his work each time depends on the unforeseeable and imponderable factors that go to make up the virtues of fidelity and sympathy, without which the work will be unrecognizable on one occasion, inert on another, and in any case betrayed.

Between the executant pure and simple and the interpreter in the strict sense of the word, there exists a difference in make-up that is of an ethical rather than of an aesthetic order, a difference that presents a point of conscience: theoretically, one can only require of the executant the translation into sound of his musical part, which he may do willingly or grudgingly, whereas one has the right to seek from the interpreter, in addition to the perfection of this translation into sound, a loving care — which does not mean, be it surreptitious or openly affirmed, a recomposition.

The sin against the spirit of the work always begins with a sin against its letter and leads to the endless follies which an ever-flourishing literature in the worst taste does its best to sanction. Thus it follows that a *crescendo*, as we all know, is always accompanied by a speeding up of movement, while a slowing down never fails to accompany a *diminuendo*. The superfluous is refined upon; a *piano, piano pianissimo* is delicately sought after; great pride is taken in perfecting useless nuances — a concern that usually goes hand in hand with inaccurate rhythm . . .

These are just so many practices dear to superficial minds forever avid for, and satisfied with, an immediate and facile success that flatters the vanity of the person who obtains it and perverts the taste of those who applaud it. How many remunerative careers have been launched by such practices! How many times have I been the victim of these misdirected attentions from abstractors of quintessences who waste time splitting hairs over a *pianissimo*, without so much as noticing egregious blunders of rendition! Exceptions, you may say. Bad interpreters should not make us forget the good ones. I agree — noting, however,

124

that the bad ones are in the majority and that the virtuosos who serve music faithfully and loyally are much rarer than those who, in order to get settled in the comfortable berth of a career, make music serve them.

The widespread principles that govern the interpretation of the romantic masters in particular, make these composers the predestined victims of the criminal assaults we are speaking about. The interpretation of their works is governed by extra-musical considerations based on the loves and misfortunes of the victim. The title of a piece becomes an excuse for gratuitous hindthought. If the piece has none, a title is thrust upon it for wildly fanciful reasons. I am thinking of the Beethoven sonata that is never designated otherwise than by the title of "The Moonlight Sonata" without anyone ever knowing why; of the waltz in which it is mandatory to find Frederick Chopin's "Farewell."

Obviously, it is not without a reason that the worst interpreters usually tackle the Romantics. The musically extraneous elements that are strewn throughout their works invite betrayal, whereas a page in which music seeks to express nothing outside of itself better resists attempts at literary deformation. It is not easy to conceive how a pianist could establish his reputation by taking Haydn as his war-horse. That is undoubtedly the reason why that great musician has not won a renown among our interpreters that is in keeping with his true worth.

In regard to interpretation, the last century left us in its ponderous heritage a curious and peculiar species of soloist without precedent in the distant past — a soloist called the orchestra leader.

It was romantic music that unduly inflated the personality of the *Kapellmeister* even to the point of conferring upon him — along with the prestige that he today enjoys on his podium, which in itself concentrates attention upon him — the discretionary power that he exerts over the music committed to his care. Perched on his sibylline tripod, he imposes his own movements, his own particular shadings upon the compositions he conducts, and he even reaches the point of talking with a naïve impudence of his specialities, of *his* fifth, of *his* seventh, the way a chef boasts of a dish of his own concoction. Hearing him speak, one thinks of the billboards that recommend eating places to automobilists: "At so-and-so's restaurant, his wines, his special dishes."

There was never anything like it in the past, in times that nevertheless already knew as well as our time go-getting and tyrannical virtuosos, whether instrumentalists or prima donnas. But those times did not yet suffer from the competition and plethora of conductors who almost to a man aspire to set up a dictatorship over music.

Do not think I am exaggerating. A quip that was passed on to me some years ago clearly shows the importance which the conductor has come to take on in the preoccupations of the musical world. One day a person who presides over the fortunes of a big concert agency was being told about the success obtained in Soviet Russia by that famous conductorless orchestra of which we have already spoken: "That doesn't make much sense," declared the person in question, "and it doesn't interest me. What I'd really be interested in is not an orchestra without a conductor, but a conductor without an orchestra."

To speak of an interpreter means to speak of a translator. And it is not without reason that a well-known Italian proverb, which takes the form of a play on words, equates translation with betrayal.

Conductors, singers, pianists, all virtuosos should know or recall that the first condition that must be fulfilled by anyone who aspires to the imposing title of interpreter, is that he be first of all a flawless executant. The secret of perfection lies above all in his consciousness of the law imposed upon him by the work he is performing. And here we are back at the great principle of submission that we have so often invoked in the course of our lessons. This submission demands a flexibility that itself requires, along with technical mastery, a sense of tradition and, commanding the whole, an aristocratic culture that is not merely a question of acquired learning.

This submissiveness and culture that we require of the creator, we should quite justly and naturally require of the interpreter as well. Both will find therein freedom in extreme rigor and, in the final analysis, if not in the first instance, success — true success, the legitimate reward of the interpreters who in the expression of their most brilliant virtuosity preserve that modesty of movement and that sobriety of expression that is the mark of thoroughbred artists.

I said somewhere that it was not enough to hear music, but that it must also be seen. What shall we say of the ill-breeding of those grimacers who too often take it upon themselves to deliver the "inner meaning" of music by disfiguring it with their affected airs? For, I repeat, one sees music. An experienced eye follows and judges, sometimes unconsciously, the performer's least gesture. From this point of view one might conceive the process of performance as the creation of new values that call for the solution of problems similar to those which arise in the realm of choreography. In both cases we give special attention to the control of gestures. The dancer is an orator who speaks a mute language. The instrumentalist is an orator who speaks an unarticulated language. Upon one, just as upon the other, music imposes a strict bearing. For music does not move in the abstract. Its translation into plastic terms requires exactitude and beauty: the exhibitionists know this only too well.

The beautiful presentation that makes the harmony of what is seen correspond to the play of sounds demands not only good musical instruction on the part of the performer, but also requires a complete familiarity on his part, whether singer, instrumentalist, or conductor, with the style of the works that are entrusted to him; a very sure taste for expressive values and for their limitations, a secure sense for that which may be taken for granted — in a word, an education not only of the ear, but of the mind.

Such an education cannot be acquired in the schools of music and the conservatories, for the teaching of fine manners is not their object: very rarely does a violin teacher even point out to his pupils that it is ill-becoming, when playing, to spread one's legs too far apart.

It is nonetheless strange that such an educational program is nowhere put into effect. Whereas all social activities are regulated by rules of etiquette and good breeding, performers are still in most cases entirely unaware of the elementary precepts of musical civility, that is to say of *musical good breeding* — a matter of common decency that a child may learn . . .

The *Saint Matthew's Passion* of Johann Sebastian Bach is written for a chamber-music ensemble. Its first performance in Bach's lifetime was perfectly realized by a total force of thirty-four musicians, including soloists and chorus. That is known. And nevertheless in our day one does not hesitate to present the work, in complete disregard of the composer's wishes, with hundreds of performers, sometimes almost a thousand. This lack of understanding of the interpreter's obligations, this arrogant pride in numbers, this concupiscence of the many, betray a complete lack of musical education.

The absurdity of such a practice is in point of fact glaring in every respect, and above all from the acoustic point of view. For it is not enough that the sound reach the ear of the public; one must also consider in what condition, in what state the sound is received. When the music was not conceived for a huge mass of performers, when its composer did not want to produce massive dynamic effects, when the frame is all out of proportion to the dimensions of the work, multiplication of the number of participant performers can produce only disastrous effects.

Sound, exactly like light, acts differently according to the distance that separates the point of emission from the point of reception. A mass of performers situated on a platform occupies a surface that becomes proportionately larger as the mass becomes more sizeable. By increasing the number of points of emission one increases the distances that separate these points from one another and from the hearer. So that the more one multiplies the points of emission, the more blurred will reception be.

In every case the doubling of parts weighs down the music and constitutes a peril that can be avoided only by proceeding with infinite tact. Such additions call for a subtle and delicate proportioning that itself presupposes the surest of tastes and a discriminating culture.

It is often believed that power can be increased indefinitely by multiplying the doubling of orchestral parts — a belief that is completely false: thickening is not strengthening. In a certain measure and up to a certain point, doubling may give the illusion of strength by effecting a reaction of a psychological order on the listener. The sensation of shock simulates the effect of power and helps to establish an illusion of balance between the sounding tonal masses. A good deal might be said in this connection about the balance of forces in the modern orchestra, a balance which is more easily explained by our aural habits than it is justified by exactness of proportions.

It is a positive fact that beyond a certain degree of extension the impression of intensity diminishes instead of increases and succeeds only in dulling the sensation.

Musicians should come to realize that for their art the same holds true as for the art of the billboard: that the blowing-up of sound does not hold the ear's attention — just as the advertising expert knows that letters which are too large do not attract the eye.

A work of art cannot contain itself. Once he has completed his work, the creator necessarily feels the need to share his joy. He quite naturally seeks to establish contact with his fellow man, who in this case becomes his listener. The listener reacts and becomes a partner in the game, initiated by the creator. Nothing less, nothing more. The fact that the partner is free to accept or to refuse participation in the game does not automatically invest him with the authority of a judge.

The judicial function presupposes a code of sanctions which mere opinion does not have at its disposal. And it is quite illicit, to my way of thinking, to set the public up as a jury by entrusting to it the task of rendering a verdict on the value of a work. It is already quite enough that the public is called upon to decide its ultimate fate.

The fate of a work, of course, depends in the final analysis on the public's taste, on the variations of its humor and habits; in a word, on its preferences. But the fate of a work does not depend upon the public's judgment as if it were a sentence without appeal.

I call your attention to this all-important point: consider on the one hand the conscious effort and patient organization that the composing of a work of art requires, and on the other hand the judgment — which is at least hasty and of necessity improvised — that follows the presentation of the work. The disproportion between the duties of the person who composes and the rights of those who judge him is glaring, since the work offered to the public, whatever its value may be, is always the fruit of study, reasoning, and calculation that imply exactly the converse of improvisation.

I have expatiated at some length on this theme in order to make you see more clearly where the true relations between the composer and the public lie, with the performer acting as an intermediary. You will thereby realize more fully the performer's moral responsibility.

For only through the performer is the listener brought in contact with the musical work. In order that the public may know what a work is like and what its value is, the public must first be assured of the

132

merit of the person who presents the work to it and of the conformity of that presentation to the composer's will.

The listener's task becomes especially harrowing where a first hearing is concerned; for the listener in this case has no point of reference and possesses no basis for comparison.

And so it comes about that the first impression, which is so important, the first contact of the new-born work with the public, is completely dependent upon the validity of a presentation that eludes all controls.

Such, then, is our situation before an unpublished work when the quality of the performers before us does not guarantee that the composer will not be betrayed and that we shall not be cheated.

In every period the forming of an elite has given us that advance assurance in matters of social relations which permits us to have full confidence in the unknown performers who appear before us under the aegis of that flawless bearing which education bestows. Lacking a guarantee of this kind, our relations with music would always be unsatisfactory. You will understand, the situation being what it is, why we have stressed at such length the importance of education in musical matters.

We have said previously that the listener was, in a way, called upon to become the composer's partner. This presupposes that the listener's musical instruction and education are sufficiently extensive that he may not only grasp the main features of the work as they emerge, but that he may even follow to some degree the changing aspects of its unfolding.

As a matter of fact, such active participation is an unquestionably rare thing, just as the creator is a rare occurrence in the mass of humanity. This exceptional participation gives the partner such lively pleasure that it unites him in a certain measure with the mind that conceived and realized the work to which he is listening, giving him the illusion of identifying himself with the creator. That is the meaning of Raphael's famous adage: to understand is to equal.

But such understanding is the exception; the ordinary run of listeners, no matter how attentive to the musical process one supposes them to be, enjoy music only in a passive way.

Unfortunately, there exists still another attitude towards music which differs from both that of the listener who gives himself up to the working out of the music — participating in and following it step by step — and from the attitude of the listener who tries docilely to go along with the music: for we must now speak of indifference and apathy. Such is the attitude of snobs, of false enthusiasts who see in a concert or a performance only the opportunity to applaud a great conductor or an acclaimed virtuoso. One has only to look for a moment at those "faces gray with boredom" as Claude Debussy put it, to measure the power music has of inducing a sort of stupidity in those unfortunate persons who listen to it without hearing it. Those of you who have done me the honor of reading the *Chronicles of My Life* perhaps recall that I stress this matter in regard to mechanically reproduced music.

The propagation of music by all possible means is in itself an excellent thing; but by spreading it abroad without taking precautions, by offering it willy-nilly to the general public which is not prepared to hear it, one lays this public open to the most deadly saturation.

The time is no more when Johann Sebastian Bach gladly traveled a long way on foot to hear Buxtehude. Today radio brings music into the home at all hours of the day and night. It relieves the listener of all effort except that of turning a dial. Now the musical sense cannot be acquired or developed without exercise. In music, as in everything else, inactivity leads gradually to the paralysis, to the atrophying of faculties. Understood in this way, music becomes a sort of drug which, far from stimulating the mind, paralyzes and stultifies it. So it comes about that the very undertaking which seeks to make people like music by giving it a wider and wider diffusion, very often only achieves the result of making the very people lose their appetite for music whose interest was to be aroused and whose taste was to be developed.

EPILOGUE

O I HAVE COME TO THE
end of my task. Permit me, before I conclude, to express the great satisfaction I feel when I think of the attention that my listeners have given me, an attention that I like to consider as the outward sign of the communion that I so eagerly wished to establish between us.

It is this communion that will be, as a kind of epilogue, the subject of the few words which I should like to say to you on the meaning of music.

We became acquainted with each other under the stern auspices of order and discipline. We have affirmed the principle of speculative volition which is at the root of the creative act. We have studied the phenomenon of music as a form of speculation in terms of sound and time. We have passed in review the formal objects of the craft of music. We took up the problem of style and looked over the biography of music. In this connection, by way of example, we followed the avatars of Russian music. Finally we examined the different problems presented by the performance of music.

In the course of these lessons I have on different occasions referred to the essential question that preoccupies the musician, just as it demands the attention of every person moved by a spiritual impulse. This question, we have seen, always and inevitably reverts back to the pursuit of the One out of the Many.

So, in concluding, I once more find myself before the eternal problem implied by every inquiry of an ontological order, a problem to which every man who feels out his way through the realm of dissimilarity — whether he be an artisan, a physicist, a philosopher, or a theologian — is inevitably led by reason of the very structure of his understanding.

Oscar Wilde said that every author always paints his own portrait: what I observe in others must likewise be observable in me. It seems that the unity we are seeking is forged without our knowing it and establishes itself within the limits which we impose upon our work. For myself, if my own tendency leads me to search for sensation in all its freshness by discarding the warmed-over, the hackneyed — the specious, in a word — I am none the less convinced that by ceaselessly varying the search one ends up only in futile curiosity. That is why I find it pointless and dangerous to over-refine techniques of discovery. A curiosity that is attracted by everything betrays a desire for quiescence in multiplicity. Now this desire can never find true nourishment in endless variety. By developing it we acquire only a false hunger, a false thirst: they are false, in fact, because nothing can slake them. How much more natural and more salutary it is to strive towards a single, limited reality than towards endless division!

Will you say this is tantamount to singing the praises of monotony?

The Areopagite maintains that the greater the dignity of the angels in the celestial hierarchy, the fewer words they use; so that the most elevated of all pronounces only a single syllable. Is that an example of the monotony we must guard against?

In truth, there is no confusion possible between the monotony born of a lack of variety and the unity which is a harmony of varieties, an ordering of the Many.

"Music," says the Chinese sage Seu-ma-tsen in his memoirs, "is what unifies." This bond of unity is never achieved without searching and hardship. But the need to create must clear away all obstacles. I think at this point of the gospel parable of the woman in travail who "hath sorrow, because her hour is come: but as soon as she is delivered of the child, she remembereth no more the anguish, for joy that a man is born into the world." How are we to keep from succumbing to the irresistible need of sharing with our fellow men this joy that we feel when we see come to light something that has taken form through our own action?

For the unity of the work has a resonance all its own. Its echo, caught by our soul, sounds nearer and nearer. Thus the consummated work spreads abroad

141

to be communicated and finally flows back towards its source. The cycle, then, is closed. And that is how music comes to reveal itself as a form of communion with our fellow man — and with the Supreme Being.